CONTEMPORARY CHRISTIAN WRITERS

IS VOLUME

117

OF THE

Twentieth Century Encyclopedia of Catholicism

UNDER SECTION

XI

CATHOLICISM AND LITERATURE

IT IS ALSO THE

112TH

VOLUME IN ORDER OF PUBLICATION

Edited by HENRI DANIEL-ROPS of the Académie Française.

CONTEMPORARY CHRISTIAN WRITERS

By *JOSEPH R. FOSTER*

HAWTHORN BOOKS · PUBLISHERS · *New York*

First Edition, November, 1963

NIHIL OBSTAT

Joannes M. T. Barton, S.T.D., L.S.S.

Censor Deputatus

IMPRIMATUR

Georgius L. Craven

Episcopus Sebastopolis, Vic. Cap.

Westmonasterii, die XX SEPTEMBRIS MCMLXIII

H-9536

018364

CONTENTS

AUTHOR'S NOTE

I should like to express my gratitude to all those who have helped me, with advice and information, to compile this little book. My thanks are particularly due to Herr S. A. Bergmann, Mr R. Hindmarsh, Professor R. O. Jones, Professor D. E. S. Maxwell, Professor A. A. Parker, Senhor L. de S. Rebelo and my brother-in-law, Mr Griffin Taylor. I alone, of course, remain responsible for the book's deficiencies.

J.R.F.

INTRODUCTION

The phrase "Christian Literature" covers a multitude of evils.
This book is concerned solely with imaginative literature that
interprets life in Christian terms. Since other books in this
series deal with poetry and the theatre, it concentrates on
prose literature, and in the period it covers—roughly 1900 to
the present—that means very largely (though by no means
entirely) the novel. It makes no attempt to deal with writers
who belong rather to the realm of philosophy or theology
than to that of literature—writers such as Theodor Haecker
and Romano Guardini in Germany, Simone Weil and Teilhard
de Chardin in France, or the Russian Berdyaev—nor is it
seriously concerned to analyse the part played by Christianity
in the work of writers like James Joyce who, although
obviously influenced by Christianity or by some particular
outward manifestation of it (in Joyce's case, Irish Catholicism), are not writing from a Christian point of view.

There are many whose hackles rise at the notion of
"Christian literature"; "a novel or a poem is either literature
or it is not," they protest; "the adjective is redundant and
meaningless." This may well have been true when Christianity
was taken for granted in Europe; but it has not been true
since the "crisis of the European conscience" at the end of
the seventeenth century. If a good deal of eighteenth-century
French literature can properly be described as anti-Christian
—and it obviously can—we must allow that the writer who
takes the opposite view writes Christian literature. As
Reinhold Schneider has pointed out, the question whether
there is such a thing as Christian literature provokes the
second question, are there writers who believe in Christ? If
so, and there clearly are, then there is also Christian literature.

Just what literature itself is has never yet been decided to everyone's satisfaction, and probably never will be, but it must surely contain two elements: it must be an objectively truthful reflection of life, that is, one that rings true to a representative number of readers, and it must inevitably, if only implicitly, reflect the author's attitude to life, that is, it must be an interpretation of life. This interpretative element may be extremely slight—it will be, for example, in an anecdotal short story, which simply aims at increasing our awareness by putting a tiny incident in sharp focus—and in the novel or play it will be implied more than stated—if the writer wished simply to make a number of statements about life he would have chosen to write a sermon or a moral discourse instead—but it will always be present to some extent. It follows that the work of a Christian writer is bound to be coloured by his beliefs and that we are entitled to call it Christian literature. François Mauriac has claimed that he is not a Catholic novelist, but a Catholic who writes novels (Graham Greene and Jean Cayrol have said the same thing); one can see what he means, but in the last analysis this is surely only a quibble. If a writer's Christianity does not affect his work decisively, it must be that his acceptance of Christianity is something less than whole-hearted. A case in point is Ford Madox Ford, who seems to have become a Catholic to please his relations, and whose attitude to Christianity in his novels is equivocal.

This brings us to the question whether it is permissible to apply non-literary standards to literature. The Christian must reply that for him at least it is, unpopular though this may make him with the school of thought which takes the view that a book must be judged purely as literature. He has the support of T. S. Eliot, who has said: "The 'greatness' of literature cannot be determined solely by literary standards; though we must remember that whether it is literature or not can be determined only by literary standards."[1] The reservation is an important one. In fact, the "literature-is-literature"

[1] *Religion and Literature*, in *Selected Prose*, Penguin Books, 1953, p. 32.

school is inconsistent, for it also maintains that if literature is to have any claim to greatness it must exhibit a high moral seriousness; in other words, this school admits that literature contains a didactic element. In plain English, the suggestion is that Christianity is to be superseded as a guide to life by the best literature. To state the case like this is a simplification, of course, for much of the best literature is in any case Christian in tone. Even so, it is a position which the Christian cannot accept; for him, Christianity is something greater than literature: as Elisabeth Langgässer puts it, "Christianity lies athwart the classical world, the world of the arts, of aestheticism, of literature; it lies athwart them and over-strides every domain that is not its own."[2] There have almost certainly been saints who could not read; and if there have not, there could have been: Graham Greene's Mexican peasants, for example, in *The Lawless Roads*, who kneel in their blue dungarees "and hold out their arms, minute after minute, in the attitude of the crucifixion; ... This is the atmosphere of the stigmata, and you realize suddenly that perhaps *this* is the population of heaven—these aged, painful and ignorant faces: they are human goodness."

If Christianity thus encompasses literature, as an important human activity, but only one among many, what is the function of the Christian writer? In essence, the answer is that he gives the abstract truths of Christianity concrete form. François Mauriac describes himself as "a metaphysician who works in the concrete. Thanks to a certain gift of atmosphere, I try to make perceptible, tangible and odorous the Catholic universe of evil. I make incarnate that sinner of whom the theologians give an abstract idea."[3]

But there is more to it than that. Important though systematization of its beliefs has been to Christianity—the unimpaired vitality of the Catholic Church is a living proof of this—it is one of the paradoxes of Christianity that it is more than a system; indeed, it might almost be described as

[2] *Das Ärgernis des Bösen* in Frankfurter Hefte, 5 Jg., 1950.
[3] *Journal* II, p. 110.

also an anti-system. Christ said with some emphasis that the spirit is more important than the letter; and his treatment of the woman taken in adultery illustrates what he meant. There must be rules; but they will always be broken; it could not be otherwise in a world which God became man to save. In such a world, Christian literature has more to do than merely test the components of life against a sort of printed circuit, rejecting them when they are defective. Mauriac illustrates the point when he says in his *Mémoires intérieures*:

> The religious life does not curb, rather does it satisfy the poetic craving, not like a fairy-tale which might be true, but like a coherent vision of existence, while, at the same time, leaving a sufficient margin of uncertainty, mystery and darkness to maintain that element of disquiet without which there could be no art, if, as I believe, every great work is an attempt to provide an answer to (the questions) "What are we? Whence do we come? Whither are we going?" (Trans. Gerard Hopkins).

Here, too, is the answer to those who would circumscribe the Christian writer's subject matter. To quote Mauriac once more, "Nothing can prevent sin being the element of the man of letters and the passions of the heart the bread and wine on which he feeds every day."[4] Julien Green goes even further:

> A novel is made of sin as a table is made of wood. Nothing pure leaves our hands, but the sin can be useful. I speak, of course, of the novel which is not written to edify. The edifying novel is usually written by the devil. Then it is a much more serious affair. We shall never know the harm this kind of literature may have done.[5]

These are some of the problems bound up with the notion of "Christian literature"; they will perhaps emerge more clearly and in various different lights during the course of the survey of individual writers which follows. It concentrates on exposition rather than criticism, but does not renounce the latter entirely.

[4] *L'Homme et le Péché*, Plon, 1938.
[5] *Le bel Aujourd'hui, 1955–1958*, Paris, 1958, p. 111.

On the whole, quotations are in English, and the names of foreign books are given in English as well as in the original (actual titles of published translations are in italics); but I have assumed that all readers will have at least a nodding acquaintance with French.

CHAPTER I

ENGLAND

Christian literature in England in the early years of this century means G. K. Chesterton and Hilaire Belloc. They met as young men and fought so many battles of ideas together that Shaw nicknamed the pair of them the "Chesterbelloc". They were both prolific writers who essayed almost every branch of literature, usually with the aim of spreading their revolutionary (or, in the eyes of their opponents, reactionary) ideas. They might almost be described as Christian encyclopedists; and, as with Voltaire and other French eighteenth-century writers, their monuments are their writings as a whole rather than masterpieces in any particular genre.

HILAIRE BELLOC

The older of the two was Joseph Peter René Hilaire Belloc (1870–1953), who was born at Saint-Cloud, near Paris; his father was a French barrister, his mother English. He was educated at the Oratory School, Birmingham, under Cardinal Newman, and Balliol College, Oxford. Belloc became a naturalized Englishman in 1902, but he always had a special affection for France and insisted on doing his military service with the French artillery. His romantic admiration for the French army must have suffered a considerable blow in 1940 and gives some of his work a dated look now. Like Chesterton, Belloc was perhaps fundamentally a journalist (in the best sense of the term); from 1906–10 he was literary editor of the *Morning Post*, in 1911 he founded the *Eye Witness* (in collaboration with G. K. Chesterton's brother, Cecil, with whom he took a leading part in attacking the politicians involved in the Marconi scandal), and much of his sociological writing first appeared in the numerous journals to which he contributed over a period of fifty years or more.

Belloc published well over a hundred books, which may be divided—very roughly—into history, sociology, essays (including travel books like *The Path to Rome* and controversial writing) and verse.

It may be that his verse will prove to be the most lasting part of his work. His light verse, especially the *Cautionary Tales*, have already given pleasure to more than one generation and will no doubt delight many more. The best of his serious verse is probably contained in the simple but deeply-felt lyrics that reflect his love for the English countryside, such as *The Evenlode* or *Ha'nacker Mill* (which he set to music himself). Belloc's sociological writing is moulded by the idea that the modern industrialized state, whether it called itself capitalist or socialist, had robbed men of freedom and responsibility; his remedy was "distributism"—"the restoration of liberty through the distribution of property", property being taken to include shares in industrial and financial enterprises. Belloc returned to this theme, which was adumbrated in the papal encyclical *Rerum Novarum* (1880), throughout his life, but it is summed up in *The Servile State* (1912), a book which reflects the close links between Belloc's historical and sociological thinking: they are both based on an outlook which has been succinctly described as "Catholic humanism".

The Servile State begins with a historical survey which suggests that the trouble began in the sixteenth century when the Church lands were seized by the crown and in great part handed out as rewards to the landed gentry, who thus came to own nearly half the agricultural land of Britain, and soon to dominate parliament. The force of the Church had been broken; a succession of weak monarchs now put the crown, too, at the mercy of the landowners. In Belloc's view this was the origin of capitalism, which concentrates money and power in the hands of comparatively few men and leads to the Servile State. Socialism is no remedy; it merely puts power into the hands of officials: "The effect of Socialist doctrine upon Capitalist society, is to produce a third thing;—to wit, the Servile State." It is one thing to analyse how things went wrong, but another to try to put the clock back, and both Belloc and Chesterton, who supported distributism, have acquired the reputation of being *laudatores tempori acti* who looked back at the Catholic Middle Ages as a sort of Golden Age. They have been called "the last of the medievalists". The fact remains that we hear a lot today of the importance of making England a "property-owning" democracy, and that Belloc's analyses of modern man are almost as relevant today as when they were written. He said in the essay called "The Modern Man" that its subject had no property, no religion, no clear sense of values and no sense of right and wrong. In so far as the picture has changed, it has changed in the direction suggested by Belloc, though the "property" is more often a television set or a refrigerator than a house or a piece of land. The decline in the value attributed to all this side of Belloc's work is due to the writer's renunciation of an active rôle in public affairs rather than to any convincing demonstration that Belloc's views were false. Both Belloc and Chesterton took part in the political life of their day; for some years Belloc was a Liberal Member of Parliament. Greene and Mauriac[1] are more concerned with the individual than with society; Waugh has pointed from a distance to its follies, but made no constructive suggestion for its improvement.

As well as sociology, Belloc also wrote an immense amount of history (he took a first in history at Oxford). His historical work includes studies of figures in English and French history—*Wolsey* (1930), *Cranmer* (1931); *Joan of Arc* (1929), *Richelieu* (1929), *Robespierre* (1901)—a *History of England* (1925–1932), and books like *Europe and the Faith* (1920) and *How the Reformation Happened* (1928). Belloc saw history

[1] Although since the Second World War Mauriac has turned himself into an effective political columnist.

in terms of personality, and he writes with considerable psychological insight and in splendid prose, but he tends to simplify issues, attributing too much influence, for example, to the power of money. Similarly, in *The Jews* (1922; new edition, 1937), he mars an otherwise sensible treatment of the subject, which he rightly regards as a problem that should not be disregarded, by reducing Communism to a Jewish-directed movement: "the Revolution now advancing in Europe is a part of the Jewish problem." Statements like "Europe is the faith, and the faith is Europe", in *Europe and the Faith*, have laid him open to the charge of attributing too much importance to temporal institutions; so much space is given to the civilizing rôle of the Church that its spiritual aspect is almost forgotten.

For all that, Belloc is a unique figure in English literature. With his French ancestry and sympathy for Latin civilization, he was able to put his readers in touch with a European Catholic tradition from which they had been cut off since the Reformation. This extract from his travel book, *The Path to Rome* (1902), which, like the later *Cruise of the "Nona"* (1925), is a collection of thoughts on life as well as a record of outward impressions, gives an oblique indication of his strength and his limitations:

> I knew a man once that was given to drinking, and I made up this rule for him to distinguish between Bacchus and the Devil. To wit: that he should never drink what has been made and sold since the Reformation—I mean especially spirits and champagne. Let him (said I) drink red wine and white, good beer and mead—if he could get it—liqueurs made by monks, and, in a word, all those feeding, fortifying, and confirming beverages that our fathers drank in old time; but not whisky nor brandy, nor sparkling wines, nor absinthe, nor the kind of drink called gin. This he promised to do, and all went well.

Belloc was not really a novelist, but he did write a number of satirical works cast in the form of novels; the best of them is *Emmanuel Burden* (1904), among whose characters is Mr I. Z. Barnett, later to become Lord Lambeth, the great

Builder of Empire from Frankfort (and by implication a Jew), whose revolutionary Haymarket Bank, which paid eight per cent on current accounts, was ruined by venomous suggestions that the interest was paid "out of the new capital daily furnished to the concern". These satirical novels were illustrated by Belloc's lifelong friend, G. K. Chesterton.

G. K. CHESTERTON

Gilbert Keith Chesterton (1874–1936) was born in Kensington; he was the son of an estate agent whose firm's name can still be seen on boards advertising property for sale by anyone walking from Paddington into the West End of London. He was educated at St Paul's School, where one of his closest friends was E. C. Bentley, who later invented the clerihew and summed up Hilaire Belloc in this one:

> Mr Hilaire Belloc
> Is a case for legislation ad hoc.
> He seems to think nobody minds
> His books being all of different kinds.

From St Paul's, Chesterton went on to the Slade School of Art, but although he had a considerable talent for drawing, ideas were his real passion and he soon began to make a name for himself as a free-lance journalist. This was the period of the Boer War; Chesterton was against the war, not because he was a pacifist, but because he considered England's attack on the Dutch farmers of the Transvaal and the Orange Free State unjustified. Chesterton heartily disliked imperialism; he gave his dislike literary form a few years later in the fantastic novel *The Napoleon of Notting Hill Gate*, which appeared in the same year as Belloc's *Emmanuel Burden*. There were many other things about Edwardian England that Chesterton disliked—the inequalities, the drift towards socialism and regimentation—and he attacked most of the intellectual leaders of the day in a series of articles and essays which were collected in 1905 in the book *Heretics*. *Heretics* deals with, among others, Rudyard Kipling, H. G. Wells, the rationalist ex-priest Joseph McCabe and Bernard Shaw, with whom Chesterton was crossing swords to the end of his life. The title *Heretics* implies that there must be some kind of orthodoxy; for Chesterton it was Christianity, which he expounded and defended in a book called simply *Orthodoxy* (1908), by which he meant not the doctrine of any particular Church—he did not become a Catholic until 1922—but "the Apostles' Creed, as understood by everybody calling himself Christian until a very short time ago and the general historic conduct of those who held such a creed". Chesterton's case for Christianity is based on logic and—something new—pressed home with humour. His favourite offensive weapon is the paradox.

Paradox can be extremely irritating when it is used to excess and degenerates into a mere verbal trick, and it certainly did very often with Chesterton; for example, when he writes in his *Autobiography* (1936), "Perhaps (this) explains why so many successful men are dull—or why so many dull men are successful". One feels that the last clause is added as an automatic afterthought. Indeed, Chesterton's paradoxes so irritated that high-minded Anglican Platonist Dean Inge that he once described Chesterton (who in later life was so mountainous that he could hardly dress or shave himself) as "that obese mountebank, who crucifies Truth head downwards". But with Chesterton paradox is much more than a verbal trick; it is at the very root of his thought. He describes in his autobiography how he once wrote in an article for a newspaper "Clapham, like every other city, is built on a volcano", and had "Clapham" altered to "Kensington" by a sub-editor who lived in Clapham and could not understand that the sentence was meant to praise, not denigrate, Clapham.

> The Clapham journalist, who glowered at me [wrote Chesterton] has been the problem of my life. He has haunted me at every turn and corner like a shadow, as if he were a blackmailer or a murderer. It was against him that I marshalled the silly halberdiers of Notting Hill and all the rest. In other words, everything I have thought and done grew originally out of that

problem which seemed to me a paradox. ... It was the problem
of how men could be made to realize the wonder and splendour
of being alive, in environments which their own daily criterion
treated as dead-alive, and which their imagination had left for
dead.

Chesterton wrote in paradoxes because he thought that the
ultimate nature of truth, including Christianity, lay in paradox; it was his way of saying what Pascal expresses in his
description of man as a thinking reed, and what Goethe had
in mind in his notion of polarity.

It was this mode of thought which inclined Chesterton to
the fantasia: *The Napoleon of Notting Hill Gate* was followed
by *The Man who was Thursday* (1908) and *The Ball and the
Cross* (1909). *The Man who was Thursday* is the story of a
policeman who enrols in a society of anarchists, only to dis-
cover that the other members of the society are in the same
position as himself. The President of the Anarchist Council
turns out to be the Chief of Police, who eventually explains
to his bewildered subordinates:

> Why does each small thing in the world have to fight against
> the world itself? ... For the same reason that I had to be alone
> in the dreadful Council of the Days. So that each thing that
> obeys law may have the glory of isolation of the anarchist.
> So that each man fighting for order may be as good and brave
> as the dynamiter.... No agonies can be too great to buy the
> right to say to this accuser [Satan], We also have suffered.

It was suggested by some critics that the President, Sunday,
was a blasphemous version of the Creator; Chesterton himself
replied in his autobiography that he was not so much God,
but rather "Nature as it appears to the pantheist, whose
pantheism is struggling out of pessimism". The story thus
marks an important stage in the development of Chesterton's
thought.

Paradox plays an important part, too, in the Father Brown
stories, that long series of detective stories (the first collection,
The Innocence of Father Brown, appeared in 1911; the last,
The Scandal of Father Brown, in 1935) whose hero was

suggested by (though hardly modelled on) Monsignor John O'Connor of Bradford, the priest who received Chesterton into the Catholic Church. Father Brown usually solves the mystery by noticing some ordinary fact that is normally over-looked: that waiters look like diners; that when people say that no one went up to a house they are probably not including the postman, whose visit is taken for granted; or that dogs howl because they have lost their toy, not because they are endowed with second sight. Like everything that Chesterton wrote, the Father Brown stories are full of Chesterton (Ronald Knox remarked that his *Short History of England* was a brilliant *résumé*, but a history of Chesterton rather than of England), and the moral is often as important as the solution of the crime. When we come across passages like this:

"'I'm afraid I'm a practical man,' said the doctor with gruff humour, 'and I don't bother much about religion and philosophy.'

'You'll never be a practical man till you do,' said Father Brown," we can see that there is at least as much of Chesterton as of Monsignor O'Connor in the dumpy little priest with his "round face under a round hat" and his old umbrella. There is no attempt at detailed realism in these stories—Father Brown pops up all over the world just at the right moment—but the setting is often clearly visualized and reminds us that Chesterton was a painter as well as an artist.

On the whole, these tales maintain a very high standard, and it seems likely that Father Brown will be the only one of the many fictional detectives of the twenties and thirties to rival the lasting fame of Sherlock Holmes.

The place occupied in Hilaire Belloc's work by history is occupied in Chesterton's by his studies in English literature. One of his first books was *Browning* (1903), and it was followed over the years by *Charles Dickens* (1906), *William Blake* (1910), *The Victorian Age in Literature* (1913), *William Cobbett* (1925), *Robert Louis Stevenson* (1927) and *Chaucer* (1932). Of course, Chesterton tended to use his subjects as pegs for his own ideas, but this really means only that he chose writers for whom he had a particular sympathy; the result is that although these books can be faulted by the pedantic scholar—for one thing, Chesterton tended to quote from memory and to bother rarely less about perfect accuracy than he might have done—they are distinguished by considerable insight and can still be read with profit. The best of these studies are probably those of Dickens and Cobbett, a man whose concern for rural England was clearly bound to make a particular appeal to Chesterton the medievalist (though it should be emphasized that Chesterton's fondness for pre-industrial England was based on sound reasoning; it was a preference for a different concept of society, not the vague nostalgia of the German Romantics).

Altogether, Chesterton published over eighty books; so far we have not mentioned his studies of saints (*St Francis of Assisi*, 1923; *St Thomas Aquinas*, 1933, which provoked the famous Thomist Etienne Gilson to say, "Chesterton makes one despair. I have been studying St Thomas all my life and I could never have written such a book"), his many volumes of essays on every subject under the sun, or his verse, the best of which (in a serious vein) is probably the long *Ballad of the White Horse* (1911), which tells the story of King Alfred's successful struggle against the Danish King Guthrum, and *Lepanto*, which has gained a place in most anthologies of twentieth-century poetry.

It is difficult to say what Chesterton's final place in English literature will be. He was a sort of Christian Voltaire (the notion would no doubt have amused him), more interested in ideas than the form in which they were expressed.

It is even possible to draw a parallel between the prose these two very different men wrote; they both have a preference for the short, brisk statement, and in particular for the unit consisting of two short statements hinged on a colon or semi-colon. Chesterton's style is less epigrammatic, but his thought moves in the same way. "Our grandmothers were quite right," he says in the chapter on "The Paradoxes of

Christianity" in *Orthodoxy*, "when they said that Tom Paine and the free-thinkers unsettled the mind. They do. They unsettled mine horribly. The rationalist made me question whether reason was of any use whatever; and when I had finished Herbert Spencer I had got as far as doubting (for the first time) whether evolution had occurred at all."

There is another parallel, too, between Voltaire and Chesterton: they both developed a new genre for the expression of their ideas; Voltaire the *conte*, Chesterton the fantastic novel. Writers who are closely concerned with the climate of ideas in their own day are bound to suffer an eclipse as the climate changes and their own ideas are either adopted or superseded. This has happened to some extent to both Voltaire and Chesterton (an entertaining guide to the climate of ideas in Chesterton's day, by the way, is his own autobiography). But writers of this calibre must always have something to say of relevance to any age. In Chesterton's case, as good an example as any is *Orthodoxy*, which is almost as penetrating an apology for Christianity as Pascal's *Pensées*, and certainly, if only because its author had time to complete it, a more cogent one. It also disposes of the idea that Chesterton was a blind optimist who disregarded the more unpleasant aspects of life. Chesterton's Christianity was based on a rigidly logical analysis of the facts; if he seems to enjoy life too much, that is only because he considered that it was normal to enjoy life. He admired the Church as the great exponent of normality; he knew that she had not found it easy to steer a safe course between the rocks and shoals of innumerable heresies; and there is no reason to suppose that he had found it any easier than the rest of us to achieve normality as an individual. He was simply certain that in the last analysis to live is better than not to live.

MAURICE BARING

There is a portrait by James Gunn of Chesterton and Belloc sitting opposite each other at a small, round table. Chesterton, in his famous cloak, is making a sketch in a note-book. Behind him, and looking over his shoulder, stands a third Catholic writer of the same generation, Maurice Baring. Baring is a very different proposition from the other two. Chesterton and Belloc were free-lance professional writers in revolt against the England of their time; Maurice Baring (1874–1945) was for six years a member of the Foreign Service and his novels—*C* (1924), *Cat's Cradle* (1925), *Daphne Adeane* (1926)—deal with the upper-class society which circulated before the First World War between London, the country and the capitals and spas of Europe.

Blanche Clifford, the heroine of *Cat's Cradle* (1925), is the daughter of a gentleman of leisure with just enough means to indulge his taste for gracious living. She falls in love with an impecunious young Army Officer, but is persuaded by her father to break off the engagement when she receives a proposal of marriage from a wealthy Italian prince, Guido Roccapalumba. Guido is in love with Blanche, who is a girl of considerable beauty and indeed, in the upshot, comes to be something of a *femme fatale*, but Blanche is not in love with him. Their life together in Guido's Roman palace, under the eagle eye of Guido's mother, is not happy. Blanche plays her part as a Roman princess with grace and correctness, but Guido knows she does not love him and is eventually stricken by a sort of nervous paralysis. Blanche has by now become a Catholic, not as a result of pressure from her husband or his mother, but because she has come to recognize in the Catholic Church something she never felt in the Anglican churches which she attended as a girl: "the presence of reality—the only reality; the eternal, the everlasting, the supernatural.... The beauty of that first Mass she went to as a Catholic was to shine before her like a lamp for the rest of her life."

Blanche looks after her paralysed husband with exemplary devotion, but eventually she falls in love with Bernard Lacy, a young English Catholic aristocrat visiting Rome. Guido senses what has happened and orders her to leave the house for good.

Years pass; Blanche keeps house for her father's widowed brother—the black sheep of the family, and a Catholic—and brings up his daughter, Rose Mary. Blanche and Bernard Lacy, still a bachelor, are thrown together again in London. Blanche still loves Bernard; Bernard still admires Blanche, but, without realizing it, falls in love with her young cousin, Rose Mary. News of Guido's death arrives from Rome. Bernard comes to tell Blanche he has made up his mind to marry Rose Mary; Blanche at first thinks he means to propose to her, realizes her mistake, but is too much in love with Bernard to clarify the situation. Bernard is too much of a gentleman to disappoint Blanche, and they marry ("quietly at the Oratory"). Rose Mary marries Bernard's great friend, Walter Troumestre, and the two couples settle down in neighbouring houses in the country. But only Walter is perfectly happy, for Bernard is unconsciously in love with Rose Mary, Blanche is eaten up with jealousy because she knows it, and Rose Mary regards her much older cousin with cold hatred for stealing Bernard from her.

To cut a long and leisurely story short (the book has 720 pages), Blanche dies of a broken heart, Walter courts and meets death as a war correspondent in the Balkans, and Bernard and Rose Mary marry. But when we leave them on the eve of the Great War, the author implies that their happiness will be overshadowed by the memory of Blanche.

There is much in this long novel which foreshadows certain aspects of Evelyn Waugh's novels; we feel that some of these idle Catholic aristocrats might have been happier had they been less heavily insulated from the material difficulties of life. Blanche's religion does not save her from unhappiness, but it does enable her to know herself—her beauty is, in a sense, the cross she has to bear through life, for she never lacks admirers—and to die at peace with herself. The moral of the story is, in Baring's own words,

"Be good, sweet maid, and let who can be clever." For Baring goes out of his way in the introduction to champion the view that there is a didactic element in art; "it always seemed to me", he says, "that if life has a moral (which it never seems to be without) and if art be the reflection of life, art must have a moral too."

In some respects, *Cat's Cradle* has dated, but the treatment of Blanche is extremely perceptive; Baring shows a remarkable grasp of feminine psychology. His model Catholic aristocrat, Lady Alice Troumestre, who "had been brought up in the school of an old-fashioned generation of Catholics, who were taught to master their feelings and to efface 'self' " embodies an ideal which recurs in Waugh's Gervaise Crouchback.

C. S. LEWIS

A writer who was decisively influenced by Chesterton is the Cambridge professor of English, C. S. Lewis (b. 1898), who has told the story of his passage "from Atheism to Christianity" in *Surprised by Joy* (1955). "In reading Chesterton," says Lewis, "I did not know what I was letting myself in for. A young man who wishes to remain a sound Atheist cannot be too careful of his reading. There are traps everywhere—'Bibles laid open, millions of surprises,' as Herbert says, 'fine nets and stratagems'. God is, if I may say it, very unscrupulous." The humorous irony of this quotation is the keynote of the most brilliant of the many books in support of Christianity which Lewis has written since his re-conversion. In *The Screwtape Letters* (1942) he took the epistolary form of *Les Liaisons dangereuses* and other eighteen-century novels, and turned it to a rather different purpose. The thirty-one letters purport to be advice from an under-secretary in Hell, a devil called Screwtape, to his nephew Wormwood, a young tempter working on a "patient" who finally evades his clutches by dying—in an air-raid—in a state of grace. Lewis makes use of this original form to paint a picture of human life vivid enough to make the most confirmed atheist wonder whether sin does not exist after all. The psychology is acute: for example, in this passage, in Letter X, on making the wrong kind of friends: "Did he commit himself deeply?

I don't mean in words. There is a subtle play of looks and tones and laughs by which a mortal can imply that he is of the same party as those to whom he is speaking. That is the kind of betrayal you should specially encourage, because the man does not fully recognize it himself; and by the time he does you will have made withdrawal difficult."

For all the seductive charm of their style, *The Screwtape Letters* are rigidly intellectual in their approach, and there are many side-kicks at sloppy thinking:

> Once humans still knew pretty well when a thing was proved and when it was not; and if it was proved they really believed it. . . . But what with the weekly press and other such weapons we have largely altered that. Your man has been accustomed, ever since he was a boy, to have a dozen incompatible philosophies dancing about together inside his head. He doesn't think of doctrines as primarily "true" or "false", but as "academic" or "practical", "outworn" or "contemporary", "conventional" or "ruthless". Jargon, not argument, is your last ally in keeping him from the Church.

The positive side of Lewis's Christianity is present in *The Screwtape Letters*, but it comes out most clearly in his more conventional books on Christianity, *Broadcast Talks, Christian Behaviour* and *Beyond Personality* (all published during the Second World War and later collected in *Mere Christianity*). It is the insistence that God meant man to be happy; "Sleeping, washing, eating, drinking, making love, playing, praying, working—all these things have to be misused, to be twisted before they can become sinful." It is easy to see why Lewis thinks so highly of Chesterton, and cannot tolerate superficial criticism of him.

The Screwtape Letters are not Lewis's only attempt at a fresh approach to religious writing. In the trilogy *Out of the Silent Planet* (1938), *Perelandra* (1943, later re-christened *Voyage to Venus*) and *That Hideous Strength* (1945), he injected religion into science fiction; the result might be described as cosmological fiction. Charles Williams (*q.v.*) tried something similar in the series of novels which begins with

War in Heaven (1930). In *Out of the Silent Planet*, a philologian called Ransom is kidnapped by a scientist and a financial adventurer and taken on a trip in a space-ship to Malacandra (Mars). There he discovers that Earth is the only planet subject to the power of the devil; in the rest of the solar system God's will is accepted without demur as a matter of course. On Mars, three different kinds of rational creatures—the seal-like *hrossa*, the frog-like *pfifltriggi* and the long-legged, long-faced *séroni* all live in harmony under the rule of God's deputy, the spirit Oyarsa, who is anxious to learn from Ransom what is happening in Earth, the silent planet, cut off from communication with the rest of the universe since it has been under the sway of the Bent One. The novel might be described as a playful (but logical) attempt to see man from God's point of view. Cosmological fiction is not an easy genre to essay; this particular example of it is successful because Professor Lewis has a readable style, the ability to tell a story, a logical basis for his fantasy and a nice sense of humour. There is an amusing scene in which the fanatical but unperceptive scientist, well versed in the conventional ways of "dealing with the natives", tries to impress the highly intelligent inhabitants of Malacandra by dangling a string of Woolworth beads before them and repeating in an encouraging tone, "Pretty, pretty! See! See!"

Like all Professor Lewis's books on Christianity (as an English don he has published a good deal of literary criticism as well), *Out of the Silent Planet* springs from his vision of Christianity as a set of common-sense rules for establishing a normal relationship between man and God. The important part played by the Devil in many of his books is proof that he does not underestimate the difficulty of putting these rules into practice, while his concern with *The Problem of Pain* (1940) obviates any charge that he sees life through rose-coloured spectacles.

Professor Lewis is an Anglican, but there is little, if anything, in his books to give pause to a Catholic or indeed to a Christian of any denomination; although he is far too clear-minded to consider points of doctrine unimportant, he is always concerned only with essentials; his position may be compared to that of the Chesterton who wrote *Orthodoxy*.

RONALD KNOX

Another writer of the next generation to Chesterton who bears witness to his influence is Monsignor Ronald Knox (1888–1957), a convert to Catholicism (the process of conversion is chronicled in *A Spiritual Aeneid*, 1918) who enjoyed the same distinction (unparalleled indeed since the sixteenth century, when the circumstances were rather different) of working in Oxford both as an Anglican and as a Roman Catholic chaplain. From 1912 to 1915 he was chaplain of Trinity College, and from 1926 to 1939 chaplain to the Catholic undergraduates of the University. In one of those essays which he did so well—the easy charm of the style should not blind us to the perceptive quality of the thought— Knox (after translating the Bible, he was resigned to being known by his surname alone: "Moffatt said this, Knox said that; I had become one of those translator fellows") says: "To me Chesterton's philosophy, in the broadest sense of that word, has been part of the air I breathed, ever since the age when a man's ideas begin to disentangle themselves from his education. His paradoxes have become, as it were, the platitudes of my thought. And this was a man whose genius touched everything; he had the universal grasp of his hero, Samuel Johnson, in days when literature had become at once more multitudinous and more specialized." ("G. K. Chesterton", in *Literary Distractions*, published posthumously in 1958.) Knox's own genius touched a good many things; apart from essays on every conceivable subject (the most extended and important of these was *God and the Atom*, 1945), he produced detective stories, parodies, a book on *Enthusiasm* (it ranges from the "Corinthians' Letter to St Paul" to the Irvingites), a mass of devotional literature and, above all, a translation of the Bible. With the devotional literature we are not concerned here; it is distinguished by concreteness, directness and simplicity. For different reasons, we need not linger over the detective stories either; they are well constructed and entertainingly written, but they do not reflect the writer's philosophy to the same extent as Chesterton's.

When it comes to parody, it is a different matter; *Let Dons Delight* (1939) is a *tour de force* whose light-hearted brilliance half-conceals a theme of the first importance, treated earlier by Newman: how can a university exist without some unifying link—which should be theology—between the various different subjects that it teaches? *Let Dons Delight* is a series of conversations among the dons of an imaginary Oxford College (appropriately called Simon Magus), at intervals of fifty years from 1588 to 1938. In the sixteenth century they cannot see that it matters whether they give their loyalty to the English or the Roman Church: by 1938 they no longer know, or at any rate disagree violently about, what to teach or why. The book is presented as a series of dreams, in which the author is present but unable to make himself heard. The last conversation is not a dream, but even in this one the author is unable to gain a hearing for his own contribution to the argument; his interjections are forcibly confined to remarks such as "You don't think perhaps...." The reader is left to guess that it would be a suggestion that the loss of Christianity might have something to do with the dons' confusion. As always, Knox wears his erudition lightly; the spirit of each age is caught perfectly, but the scholarship is never obtrusive. *Let Dons Delight* must be one of the most original volumes of apologetics ever written; it is certainly one of the most polished and amusing.

The most important single literary task Knox undertook was his translation of the Bible; "nine years' hard", he calls it himself. It is "A Translation from the Latin Vulgate in the Light of the Hebrew and Greek Originals"; the New Testament appeared in 1947, the Old Testament in 1949. Knox's Bible was the first complete Catholic translation of the Bible into English to be published since Bishop Challoner revised the Douay-Rheims version in the eighteenth century. Its reception was mixed. It has not completely replaced the Douay version; whether it will be accepted for as long still remains to be seen. Perhaps from now onwards every generation will want to make its own translation of the Bible. Knox expressly avoided contemporary idiom in the hope that this would make his work more lasting. He has told us what his aim was in *On Englishing the Bible* (1949):

> In a word, what you want is neither sixteenth-century English nor twentieth-century English, but timeless English. Whether you can get it, is another question. The method I proposed to myself was this—to use no word, no phrase, and as far as possible no turn of sentence, which would not have passed as decent literary English in the seventeenth century, and would not pass as decent literary English today.

In practice, this approach led Knox to resort too frequently to inversion, especially in the Old Testament. Whatever view one takes of the Knox Bible, two things are certain: that Knox thought a good deal about the problems of translation in general and gave the most careful consideration to every word he wrote—his reasoned and usually convincing replies to criticism of specific turns are sufficient evidence of that—and that his translation forced many English Catholics to read and talk about a book which previously they had seldom taken out of their bookshelves, if they possessed it at all. In fact, few would deny that, in the case of St Paul's epistles at least, Knox made readable sense of passages which the Douay translation had left as very near nonsense. The situation today is very different from what it was when Knox started work. Biblical studies are in a flourishing state in the Catholic Church; in America the new Confraternity version is in process of publication, and France has produced the much-praised Jerusalem Bible, now in process of being translated into English.

Those who would know more of Knox, who might well be described as a twentieth-century Newman, cannot do better than turn to Evelyn Waugh's authoritative biography (*The

Life of Ronald Knox 1959), a detailed and sympathetic account of his life which also contains a full list of his published works.

CHARLES WILLIAMS

The name of Charles Williams (1886–1945) has already cropped up. Williams was an Anglo-Catholic who spent his working life in the offices of the Oxford University Press, mainly in London but also, during the Second World War, in Oxford, where he had many friends, among them C. S. Lewis. Besides the novels already mentioned, he produced a considerable amount of poetry, half-a-dozen plays, a number of biographies and a good deal of literary criticism and directly religious writing. *The Descent of the Dove: A Short History of the Holy Spirit in the Church* (1939) comes into the last category; it is notable for the honourable place in the history of Christianity which it accords to scepticism as a necessary concomitant of faith. Williams is one of the few modern Christian writers prepared to do justice to the positive side of Voltaire:

> In matters of public morals Voltaire shocked and justly shook the Church. The mechanical operation of cruelty which proceeded under the automatic rigour of the still officially Christian governments was halted, for a few brief moments, by the incredible energy of the old man of Ferney. . . . Voltaire attacked in force and with a passion of sincerity: "I will not laugh while such things are done." He wrote across the brain of all future Christendom: "Ecrasez l'nfâme!" Christendom will be unwise if ever she forgets that cry, for she will have lost touch with contrition once more. She had forgotten—or at least her rulers had forgotten—Man; the candles burned to the Incarnate, but the co-inherence of all men was being lost.

But the dominant note of Williams's work is the reverse of scepticism; it is a romantic, mystical symbolism (he wrote an unpublished book on "the outlines of Romantic theology"), a pursuit of the *Via Positiva*, which reaches its climax—or runs riot—in the difficult later poems on the Arthurian legend, *Taliessin through Logres* (1938) and *The Region of the Summer Stars* (1944), on which his friend and admirer C. S. Lewis has written a commentary in *Arthurian Torso* (1948). Williams has been compared with Blake; there certainly seems to be some correspondence between the symbolical geography of the Arthurian poems and Blake's "States". Williams himself tells us in the preface to *The Region of the Summer Stars* that Logres is Britain regarded as a province of the Empire with its centre at Byzantium. The theme of the poems is the expectation of our Lord's Return, foreshadowed in the coming of the Grail. But unity is destroyed by the strife between Lancelot and Arthur: "Logres is overthrown and afterwards becomes the historical Britain, in which the myth of its origin remains". The end-paper of *Taliessin through Logres* shows the Empire in the form of a human figure, with Logres as the head, Gaul as the breasts, Byzantium as the navel, and so on. By the time one gets to the buttocks—Caucasia—one begins to feel that this kind of symbolism can be overdone, and that it is all a far cry from any kind of reality, whether divine or human.

The same kind of feeling is aroused by Williams's novels, which reflect his early interest in a group of London Rosicrucians known as the Order of the Golden Dawn (its members included, at various times, W. B. Yeats, Arthur Machen, Algernon Blackwood and even the notorious Alistair Crowley) and in A. E. Waite's books on the occult (another influence was the Christian mysticism of the Edwardian novelist and religious writer Evelyn Underhill, whose letters Williams edited in 1943). These novels were first mentioned here in connection with those of C. S. Lewis, but in fact there is a good deal of difference between the two series. Lewis's affinities are with science fiction and scholastic philosophy; he is imaginative but coolly logical. Williams's novels, for all their high-flown symbolism, are essentially ghost stories in the tradition of Sheridan Le Fanu and M. R. James; they are often occupied with magic and the power of evil, and the general atmosphere is one of vague religiosity. The heroine of the last of them, *All Hallows' Eve* (1945) is already dead when the book opens, although we do not appreciate this at first (William Golding later used the same device in a more extreme form in *Pincher Martin*, 1956). Hovering between heaven and earth, she helps her still-living husband to defeat the machinations of a necromancer called Father Simon, or Simon the Clerk, a Jew born in Paris just before the Revolution and still (1945) going strong; indeed, more strongly than ever, for he has just divided himself into three (the duplicate and triplicate are at work in Russia and China) and he is about to send his daughter on a permanent visit to the realm of the dead (she has been doing night trips for some time), apparently to act as his agent there. It is impossible to take this sort of thing very seriously, especially as the writing alternates between the banal and the tiresomely rhapsodic, and although one or two of Williams's novels deal with themes which have a better claim to our attention we must in general agree with the sympathetic critic who describes these "metaphysical thrillers", rather defensively, as "middlebrow".

T. S. ELIOT

It is only fair to add that some people think much more highly of them, and that when *All Hallows' Eve* was reissued in 1947 it enjoyed the benefit of an introduction by a man who must certainly be regarded as one of the most important Christian writers of the last forty years, the Anglo-American Thomas Stearns Eliot (b. 1888). Eliot came to England in 1915, entered the Church of England in 1927 and was awarded the Order of Merit and the Nobel Prize for Literature in 1948. *The Waste Land* (1922) was a landmark in modern poetry, and *Murder in the Cathedral* (1935) initiated the revival of poetic drama (especially on Christian themes) which has been proceeding fitfully ever since and whose latest fruits have been the plays of Christopher Fry. However, we are not concerned here with Eliot's poetry or plays (for these, the reader is referred to the volumes in this series on poetry and the theatre), but only with his prose, which can be roughly divided into literary criticism and social criticism.

In *The Use of Poetry and the Use of Criticism* (1933), Eliot wrote, "From time to time, every hundred years or so, it is desirable that some critic shall appear to review the past of our literature, and set the poets and the poems in a new order. This task is not one of revolution but of readjustment". Eliot has himself performed this task admirably for his own generation. This is not to say that all his verdicts have been, or should be, accepted without question, or that there have not been other critics of equal stature at work in the same period, but Eliot's opinions are always well-founded and expressed coolly, clearly and cogently, and he has caused us to look with fresh eyes at Donne and the other metaphysical poets, Milton, Dryden and, in France, Baudelaire and the symbolists (to whom his own poetry owes a good deal). He defined his position as a critic in his second collection of essays, *For Lancelot Andrewes* (1928), as "classicist in literature, royalist in politics and anglo-catholic in religion," and this position he has maintained throughout his critical work. He is a traditionalist, in the best sense of the word; for Eliot, tradition does not mean following blindly what has gone before; it is something much more difficult:

> Tradition is a matter of much wider significance. It cannot be inherited, and if you want it you must obtain it by great labour. It involves, in the first place, the historical sense, which we may call nearly indispensable to anyone who would continue to be a poet beyond his twenty-fifth year; and the historical sense involves a perception, not only of the greatness of the past, but of its presence; the historical sense compels a man to write not merely with his own generation in his bones, but with a feeling that the whole of the literature of Europe from Homer and within it the whole of the literature of his own country has a simultaneous existence and composes a simultaneous order. This historical sense, which is a sense of the timeless as well as of the temporal and of the timeless and of the temporal together, is what makes a writer traditional.

And it is at the same time what makes a writer most acutely conscious of his place in time, of his own contemporaneity.

No poet, no artist of any art, has his complete meaning alone. His significance, his appreciation is the appreciation of his relation to the dead poets and artists (*Tradition and the Individual Talent*, 1919).

Christianity is the most important strand in the European tradition, and it is naturally always recurring in Eliot's critical writing. We have already referred to the essay on *Religion and Literature* (1935): its theme is so pertinent to the subject of this book that a brief analysis will not be out of place.

Eliot will have none of the attempt to make literature something to be judged in isolation on its own merits as literature alone. The essay opens with the downright statement that "Literary criticism should be completed by criticism from a definite ethical and theological standpoint". It goes on to define the nature of purely "literary" enjoyment:

> While I acknowledge the legitimacy of this enjoyment, I am more acutely aware of its abuse. The persons who enjoy these writings [Clarendon, Gibbon, Bradley, Buffon, the Authorized translation of the Bible] *solely* because of their literary merit are essentially parasites; and we know that parasites, when they become too numerous, are pests. I could fulminate against the men of letters who have gone into ecstasies over "the Bible as Literature", the Bible as "the noblest monument of English prose". Those who talk of the Bible as a "monument of English prose" are merely admiring it as a monument over the grave of Christianity.

Eliot goes on to suggest that the history of the English novel can be divided into three phases—in the first it took Christianity for granted (Fielding, Dickens, Thackeray); in the second it questioned it (George Eliot, Meredith, Hardy); in the third and present one it treats it as an anachronism— and then affirms that "the whole of modern literature is corrupted by what I call Secularism, ... it is simply unaware of, simply cannot understand the meaning of, the primacy of the supernatural over the natural life: of something which I assume to be our primary concern." The conclusion is that all Christians must consciously maintain "certain standards and criteria of criticism over and above those applied by the rest of the world . . . by these criteria and standards everything that we read must be tested."

This is necessarily a severely telescoped account of a closely reasoned and carefully balanced essay—for example, Eliot is at pains to emphasize that he does not want two literatures, one for Christians and the other for pagans—but it is perhaps sufficient to convey the stature and authority of Eliot as a critic, and the standpoint from which he writes.

BRUCE MARSHALL

The Scottish satirist Bruce Marshall (b. 1899) is in a very different class from Eliot as a writer, but he is equally concerned to emphasize "the primacy of the supernatural over the natural life". Most of his novels, which have all been deservedly successful—they are for the most part eminently readable—are decidedly *romans à thèse*; the thesis is that all will not be well with the world until it turns back to God. The trouble with Marshall is that he is so eager to make his points and, if possible, to raise a laugh as he does it, that his writing is apt to grow careless and to fall into bathos. One of the worst examples of this is the passages in *Father Malachy's Miracle* (1931) dealing with Andrew Gillespie, archly nicknamed the Bishop's Bad Brother or—worse—the Bee Bee Bee. In general, Marshall is more successful in creating saintly priests than sinful laymen; Father Malachy, the little Benedictine who successfully prays God to remove the Garden of Eden dance hall from Edinburgh to the top of the Bass Rock in the hope of impressing a sceptical Episcopalian rector and converting the British Isles, rings truer than the caricatures of business men and theatrical agents who thwart his purpose.

The truth is, I think, that Marshall is only accidentally a novelist; he uses the novel because it is the form handiest for his purpose in the twentieth century, but he is fundamentally a satirical moralist, to be compared rather with writers like Theophrastus or La Bruyère than with other novelists. This comes out very clearly if we compare *A Thread of Scarlet* (1959) with Henry Morton Robinson's *The Cardinal* (1950). The theme of both books is identical: the life of a priest from ordination to cardinal's hat. Both books are set in roughly the same period and introduce some of the same historical figures, such as Pope Pius XI. Robinson's book is a fully-realized novel of six hundred pages; Marshall's book covers the same ground in under two hundred pages and can most properly be described as a series of humorous, thumbnail scenes from the life of a Catholic cleric. It is also a sparkling piece of apologetics; coy and arch though he can be at his worst moments, Marshall is at bottom a clear thinker who faces all the facts and is not in the least sentimental. Nearer to the novel proper is *Yellow Tapers for Paris* (1943), a story of Paris (where Marshall worked up to 1940) at the time of the fall of France, though here too no pains are taken to hide the moral, namely, that France fell because too many Frenchmen had ceased to have any patriotism, religion or self-discipline.

EVELYN WAUGH

A satirist of a cooler—indeed, a positively icy—brand is Evelyn Waugh (b. 1903). The outward facts of Waugh's life are that he was born in Hampstead, educated at Lancing and Hertford College, Oxford, published his first book (a life of *Dante Gabriel Rossetti*) in 1927, was received into the Roman Catholic Church in 1930, travelled extensively in the years before the Second World War, spent most of that war in the Army, and has lived since 1937 in Gloucestershire or Somerset. His father was a publisher and literary critic, his elder brother is Alec Waugh, the author of that well-known tilt at the English public school, *The Loom of Youth*, and his son Auberon has already published a novel, the clever but juvenile *Foxglove Saga* (1960). For the inner shape of Waugh's career, we can do no better than turn to the opening pages of the semi-autobiographical *Ordeal of Gilbert Pinfold* (1957), where Waugh has outlined it in his own inimitably detached style:

> It may happen in the next hundred years that the English novelist of the present day will come to be valued as we now value the artists and craftsmen of the late eighteenth century. . . .
>
> Among these novelists Mr Gilbert Pinfold stood quite high. At the time of his adventure, at the age of fifty, he had written a dozen books all of which were still bought and read. . . . Foreign students often chose them as the subject for theses, but those who sought to detect cosmic significance in Mr Pinfold's work, to relate it to fashions in philosophy, social predicaments, or psychological tensions, were baffled by his frank, curt replies to their questionnaires; their fellows in the English literature School, who chose more egotistical writers, often found their theses more than half composed for them. Mr Pinfold gave nothing away. Not that he was secretive or grudging by nature; he had nothing to give these students. He regarded these books as objects which he had made, things quite external to himself to be used and judged by others. He thought them well made, better than many reputed works of genius, but he was not vain of his accomplishment, still less of his reputation.

Pinfold is not Waugh, but the two have a good deal in common. The most hostile of Waugh's critics have always been forced to admit that he is a very professional writer whose work is never anything less than extremely readable, and F. J. Stopp's study of him was justifiably sub-titled *Portrait of an Artist*.

It is alleged that when he was at Lancing Waugh belonged to a coterie which carried its own plush-covered lavatory seats across the quad every morning. Some critics have maintained that this kind of attitude runs through all his work, that he is, in short, a snob, writing only about the upper classes and clinging without much justification to the fading glories of English country-house life. This is a superficial view. Waugh is attracted to the aristocracy because he sees

Christianity as a historical religion and the Catholic Church as the only logical form which it can take; those families which have remained Catholic preserve a tradition—a civilization, even—that was shattered in England by the Reformation. Even the non-Catholic aristocracy (Tony Last's family in *A Handful of Dust*, for instance) embodies some of the decencies that went with the old way of life; all else is the new barbarism. This point of view may be a trifle extreme—it involves throwing overboard certain aspects of post-Reformation England which are perhaps not without value—but it is a logically defensible one. Of course, there are elements in Waugh's attitude which can only be described as a pose, but he has paraded these elements in *The Ordeal of Gilbert Pinfold* with such calculated yet engaging candour that the only possible reaction, and surely the one intended, is laughter. A good example is Pinfold's refusal to own a wireless set, so that when he wishes to hear the broadcast of an interview he has given to the B.B.C. he has to have "the cook's wireless carried into the drawing-room. He and Mrs Pinfold listened together. His voice came to him strangely old and fruity, but what he said gave him no regret. 'They tried to make an ass of me,' he said. 'I don't believe they succeeded.'"

Waugh is more than a satirist, but satire was the dominant note in his work up to *Brideshead Revisited* (1945) and one that is present to some extent in all his novels. His first was *Decline and Fall* (1928), a description of life at an imaginary preparatory school. At the time, Waugh felt obliged to state in capital letters at the end of the short preface that the book was meant to be funny. This precaution seems to have been suggested by a degree of incomprehension on the part of his publishers, but it is difficult today to imagine that anyone could not find it funny. There is an element of satire in *Decline and Fall*, but the keynote of the book is sheer unconfined mirth. Paul Pennyfeather, reading for the Church at Scone College, is debagged by the drunken members of a dining club and quite unjustly and unjustifiably expelled for indecent behaviour. He follows the advice of the college porter

("I expect you'll be becoming a schoolmaster, sir. That's what most of the gentlemen does, sir, that gets sent down for indecent behaviour.") and takes a job at Llanabba Castle, a twentieth-century Dotheboys Hall, where one of his colleagues is an engaging scoundrel called Captain Grimes (he eventually contracts a bigamous marriage with the headmaster's daughter) and the shooting of a boy in the heel with the starter's pistol at the school sports passes almost unnoticed. Paul adjusts himself to these strange conditions with surprising ease and after a series of improbable adventures, including a sojourn in prison, returns to Scone to continue his theological studies and to condemn heresies in the primitive church with a severity worthy of his creator.

Waugh tells us in the "Author's Note" which precedes *Decline and Fall* that his publishers called the book "a shocking novelette". If by this they meant that it had literally shocked them, one can understand how they felt. The first impression produced in the reader by this book and by the satirical novels that followed it in the next fifteen years (*Vile Bodies*, 1930; *Black Mischief*, 1932; *A Handful of Dust*, 1937; *Scoop*, 1938; *Put Out More Flags*, 1942) is one of disorientation. All kinds of deserving targets are hit (the futility of the social whirl in *Vile Bodies*, the absurdity of importing the superficial techniques of European civilization into Africa in *Black Mischief*, the irresponsible methods of the newspaper world in *Scoop*), but the carnage is so widespread, and the fire comes from so many different angles that it is difficult to see where (if anywhere) the author's sympathies really lie. As Mr Graham Martin puts it,[2]

> The satirical bias, which we begin by assuming is simply hidden from view by the parodic report, turns out to have no definable status. When Waugh appears to offer one, it is only a trick. He lures the reader into a judgement—in the context of neutral narration we are eager to accept one—and then

[2] *Novelists of Three Decades, Pelican Guide to English Literature,* Ed. Boris Ford, 1961 (Vol. 7, p. 398).

leaves him there, the target of hostility more subtle and more deep-seated than he had guessed.

Mr Martin also complains of Mr Waugh's "ambivalent attitude" to Basil Seal, the highly successful rotter of *Put Out More Flags*. No doubt by the standards of the most earnest academic criticism these tricks are reprehensible, but in practice they are two of the elements which gives Waugh's earlier work its unique savour. Another is the merciless nonchalance with which he treats his characters, killing them off in a few lines or delivering them up to fates even worse than death, such as perpetually reading Dickens to a madman in the Amazonian jungle (this is the lot of Tony Last, the hero of *A Handful of Dust*). The accusation of cruelty is beside the point; most of the characters in these pre-war books are only symbols or abstractions, as Waugh implies in the words he puts into the novelist hero of the unfinished novel *Work Suspended* (1942): "The algebra of fiction must reduce its problems to symbols if they are to be soluble at all. I am shy of a book commended to me on the grounds that the 'characters are alive'."

The first novel (except perhaps for the earlier part of *A Handful of Dust*) in which the characters are fully rounded creatures of flesh and blood—and in which the positive side of Waugh's Catholicism is reflected—is *Brideshead Revisited*. Originally published in 1945, it was re-issued in 1960 with, in the author's words, "many small additions and some substantial cuts". In the preface to the reissued edition, Waugh has this to say of the book:

> This novel ... lost me such esteem as I once enjoyed among my contemporaries and led me into an unfamiliar world of fan-mail and press photographers. Its theme—the operation of divine grace on a group of diverse but closely connected characters—was perhaps presumptuously large, but I make no apology for it. I am less happy about its form, whose more glaring defects may be blamed on the circumstances in which it was written.

These circumstances were the closing phases of the Second World War, and for that reason Waugh suggests that *Brideshead* should be treated as a souvenir of that war "rather than of the twenties or thirties, with which it ostensibly deals", Waugh does himself an injustice; *Brideshead* certainly is a commentary on certain angles of the war, but it is primarily a bright impressionistic picture of pre-war Oxford and other aspects of pre-war England. If it lost him readers, that is because in 1945 it seemed almost mawkish after the astringent tone of his previous books; a reading of the revised edition does not confirm this impression, even if one or two phrases remain to raise the reader's eyebrow; for example, undergraduates are described as clearing the fumes of alcohol "in puppyish romps and tumbles". The central theme is handled with the restraint to be expected from the Pinfold who "away from his parish sought the least frequented Mass" and at home "held aloof from the multifarious organizations which have sprung into being at the summons of the hierarchy to redeem the times". The agnostic Charles Ryder is introduced—quite incidentally—to Catholicism by his Oxford friend, the charming, infuriating but fundamentally tragic—and saintly—Sebastian Flyte. Friendship with Sebastian is eventually followed many years later by a love affair—when Ryder and Julia are both already married—with his sister Julia. Ryder sees their father, the reprobate Lord Marchmain, reconciled to the Church before he dies, and then learns from Julia that she is not after all prepared to divorce her husband and marry him: "I'm not quite bad enough ... to set up a rival good to God's." The effect on Charles Ryder of his long contact with the Catholic Marchmains is nowhere described; but when he returns, years later, to be billeted as an Army officer in a now deserted Brideshead (the Marchmains' house), he visits the chapel again, and this time he does not merely stare at the *art nouveau* decorations; he says a prayer, "an ancient, newly-learned form of words". The excellence of the descriptive passages and the precision of the dialogue with which the characters are created make the revised version of *Brideshead*

Revisited a book that can be read with pleasure again and again. It is also distinguished among Waugh's post-war books by complete unity of tone; it is a vision successfully committed to paper. It is unlikely to convert the man in the street to Catholicism, but it is a wonderfully convincing picture of one of those old English Catholic families which have such a hold on Waugh's imagination; he returns to the theme in the *Men at Arms* trilogy.

In the years immediately after the war Waugh reverted to satire, with *Scott-King's Modern Europe* (1947)—a tilt at the heartless tyranny of modern bureaucratic governments—and *The Loved One* (1948), a blistering attack on those American methods of dealing with the dead which deny the dignity of death by refusing to call it by its proper name. The Whispering Glades, the last resting place of the Loved Ones, is based on a real establishment of this sort in California. In these two books we are back in the unreal world of *Decline and Fall* and *Scoop*; Dennis Barlow, the secretary of the home for dead animals known as the Happy Hunting Grounds, displays much of the unscrupulous enterprise of Basil Seal, and his girl-friend, Miss Thanatogenos, when bidden to "take the elevator to the top floor, find a nice window and jump out", does just that. The very slight *Love Among the Ruins*, "a romance of the near future" (1953) is pitched in the same key; the object of Miles Plastic's affection, classically beautiful in every other way, sports a corn-coloured beard, and the most popular of the State's comprehensive welfare arrangements is the euthanasia service.

The most direct statement of Waugh's Christianity is *Helena* (1948), not one of his most successful novels but a very skilfully contrived one. It is a historical novel written in the terse and economical style of the satires with an admixture of their mordant humour (for instance, the suffocation of Constantine's wife, Fausta, in her bath) which at first seems slightly out of place but in fact has its part to play in underlining the horror of "Power without Grace", which is Waugh's summary of the Roman Empire in the last days of the pagan period.

The central theme of the novel is the importance of Christianity's historical basis. Waugh has elected to follow that version of the life of the Empress Helena which puts her birthplace in Britain, and we meet her first at the court of her father, Old King Coel, chief of the Trinovantes. She falls in love with and marries Constantius Chlorus, who takes her off to his home in the Balkans. Constantius becomes a Mithraist, and Helena, whose main characteristic is a down-to-earth bluntness, asks, à propos of the myth of Mithras, "when and where did these things happen?" She asks the same question of all the religions she encounters, and gets no satisfactory answer until she meets the Christian writer Lactantius, who can say that Christ had died two hundred and seventy-eight years before in Aelia Capitolina (Jerusalem). She becomes a Christian, and when she finds that no one knows what happened to the Cross she makes it her mission to find it. With the help of the Wandering Jew, who appears to her in a dream, she is eventually successful.

The reason why *Helena* was given a somewhat mixed reception is almost certainly that its style, for a historico-religious novel, is, as we have hinted, so original as to be at first disconcerting. But fundamentally there is no reason why weighty themes should always be treated in weighty language, and a re-reading shows, as it does so often with Waugh's later books, that the relaxed and humorous directness of the language are the product of a highly polished art which knows just what it is about.

The third of Waugh's "positively" Catholic novels is the trilogy consisting of *Men at Arms* (1952), *Officers and Gentlemen* (1955) and *Unconditional Surrender* (1961). These three books form the largest canvas that Waugh has yet attempted and it is one that comes off brilliantly. In the foreground is Guy Crouchback, scion of an old Catholic family who sees the war as a crusade in which he can make amends for a hitherto somewhat unsatisfactory life; in the background is wartime England, touched in with a series of light but skilful strokes that convey a host of acutely observed details. The book also shows us some of the fighting, for Guy's service takes him to Dakar, Crete and Yugoslavia, where he acts as liaison officer with the partisans, and the commandant of his corps, the Halberdiers, meets his comically tragic end in an unnecessary and more or less single-handed attack on a minor German position.

Most critics have regarded Guy's father, Gervaise Crouchback, the old Catholic aristocrat who sells up the ancestral home and ends his days living humbly in a seaside hotel, as, so to speak, Waugh's "ideal Christian". He is certainly presented as "a just man in the full sense of the psalmist", but the claims of Guy himself should not be dismissed out of hand. His supreme action is his reconciliation with his wife, the promiscuous Virginia, in the full knowledge that she is soon to bear another man's child. Also to his credit are his efforts to save a couple of Jewish refugees in Yugoslavia, and his unquestioning continuation of the numerous pensions his father had been paying to various impoverished people (even if it is relatively easy to give money away when you are still going to have plenty, or at any rate enough, left for yourself). In the *Men at Arms* trilogy, Waugh's style reaches a new pitch of refinement. The old humour is still there, but it is put over with even more economy than before, and the dialogue is admirably precise in its establishment of character. One of the best set-pieces is old Mr Crouchback's funeral at Broome, attended by a wide variety of characters, from the Lord-Lieutenant of the county to Guy's chance acquaintance, the American Lieutenant Padfield, "exercising heaven knows what prodigy of ubiquity".

Waugh has also written a number of travel books and biographies of *Edmund Campion* (1935) and *Ronald Knox* (1959). As a novelist, he has chosen to study a fairly narrow sector of society from one clearly-defined and very personal point of view, but within his self-imposed limits he shows a high degree of mastery.

GRAHAM GREENE

Although there is truth in Mr Patrick O'Donovan's remark, made in a wireless talk about English Roman Catholics, that "if you are a writer you are filed under a special, eccentric, and rather disliked category by most of the critics in the country", the fact remains that Evelyn Waugh has obliged these critics to devote a considerable share of their attention to him in the last twenty years or so, and the same is true of his contemporary and fellow-novelist, Graham Greene (b. 1904). Greene's world is a very different one from that of the writers we have considered so far, all of whom enjoy life in one way or another and reveal the fact in their books. Greene has called his less serious novels "Entertainments", but he seldom admits to being entertained himself. In an essay called *The Revolver in the Corner Cupboard* (which here and there rings, uncharacteristically, just a shade false), he has told how at the age of eighteen or so he used to play Russian roulette with a loaded revolver out of sheer boredom. This mood recurs in almost all the novels. Greene has ringed the globe with a set of characters who find life not only grim but tedious. Pinkie Brown in Brighton, Tench the dentist in Mexico, Fowler in Indo-China, Scobie and his re-incarnation, Querry, in Africa are all men who have extracted little happiness from living; in Greene's own phrase, "misery's graduates". Even their sins are sad. The mood is summed up by Scobie in *The Heart of the Matter*: "It seemed to Scobie that life was immeasurably long. Couldn't the test of man have been carried out in fewer years? Couldn't we have committed our first major sin at seven, have ruined ourselves for love or hate at ten, have clutched at redemption on a fifteen-year-old deathbed?" Pinkie had already achieved this ideal, except for the clutch at redemption.

Greene is the son of a schoolmaster; his father was the headmaster of Berkhamsted School, which Greene himself attended before going on to Balliol. He began his career as a sub-editor with *The Times*, and published his first novel, *The Man Within*, in 1929. Since then he has written some fifteen novels, three plays, two or three travel books, a certain amount of criticism, a number of short stories and the script of a very successful film, *The Third Man* (1950). His style of writing in general lends itself to adaptation for the cinema; several of the novels have been turned into effective films.

Greene's first novels may be described as psychological thrillers; indeed the themes of violence and pursuit run through all his novels. As well as being pursued by others, the central characters in these early books are in pursuit of themselves. Andrews, the hero of *The Man Within* (1929), a historical novel set in Sussex at the beginning of the nineteenth century, is a smuggler who betrays his friends to the excisemen and is persuaded by a girl in whose house he finds refuge to give evidence against them. The title of the book is taken from Sir Thomas Browne's words, "There's another man within me that's angry with me". In *A Gun for Sale* (1936), the central character, Rowen, has been hired by some armament manufacturers to assassinate the head of a European state, but the two hundred pounds he has been paid is reported to the police as stolen money and Rowen is on the run. He meets a girl whom he trusts, but in the end she is forced to betray him. Rowen has been made what he is by upbringing and environment, and to that extent he is a forerunner of Pinkie, the young gangster in *Brighton Rock*, but he does not possess Pinkie's awareness of good and evil.

Greene became a Catholic in 1926, but the first of his novels in which the conflict in the central character assumes a specifically religious form is in fact *Brighton Rock* (1938). In this novel, the American edition of which was rather curiously classified as an "Entertainment", we watch the young leader of a Brighton razor gang commit two murders and attempt a third in the full knowledge that he is damning himself for ever. Pinkie Brown is a Catholic with a clear understanding of the meaning of good and evil, but his childhood in the slums of Brighton has robbed him of the capacity to love or to envisage heaven as a real possibility: " 'Of course it's true,' the Boy said, 'what else could there be?... Of course there's Hell. Flames and damnation, torments.'

" 'And Heaven too,' Rose [the sixteen-year-old he marries in a register-office—another sin—to prevent her giving evidence against him] said with anxiety, while the rain fell interminably on.

" 'Oh, maybe,' the Boy said, 'maybe.' "

Pinkie falls over a cliff, his face burnt with vitriol; Rose is left alive to bear his child and play the dreadful gramophone record on which he has recorded his hatred of her. There are points about *Brighton Rock* that raise questions in the reader's mind (Could a non-drinking, non-smoking youth like Pinkie impose his will on grown men like Cubitt, Dallow and Spicer? Would a woman like Ida—the averagely good pagan—display the pertinacity she does in ferreting out Fred Hale's killer?), but on the whole it succeeds brilliantly in conveying a picture of the seamy, seedy side of Brighton and of what might go on in the minds of two of its products.

Greene has given us his view of the place of religion in the novel in his essay on François Mauriac, a writer by whom he has certainly been influenced, in *The Lost Childhood and Other Essays* (1951).

With the death of (Henry) James the religious sense was lost to the English novel, and with the religious sense went the importance of the human act. It was as if the world of fiction had lost a dimension: the characters of such distinguished writers as Mrs Virginia Woolf and Mr E. M. Forster wandered like cardboard symbols through a world that was paper-thin ... M. Mauriac's first importance to an English reader, therefore, is that he belongs to the company of the great traditional novelists: he is a writer for whom the visible world has not ceased to exist, whose characters have the solidity and importance of men with souls to save or lose, and a writer who claims the traditional and essential right of a novelist, to comment, to express his views.

Greene speaks here from a purely literary standpoint; elsewhere[3] he has made it plain that he will have nothing to do with the view that in the last analysis literature must be judged by extra-literary standards:

> There are leaders of the Church who regard literature as a means to one end, edification. That end may be of the highest value, of far higher value than literature, but it belongs to a different world. Literature has nothing to do with edification.

Of course, the word "edification" has overtones which confuse the issue; no one would want a novelist to try to write deliberately edifying books; but this does not invalidate the demand that in the last resort books must be judged by the standards by which we have decided to live our lives; that is, in the case of a Christian, by Christian standards.

In the same essay Greene emphasizes that it is the writer's privilege to be disloyal to his political or religious group:

> I belong to a group, the Catholic Church, which would present me with grave problems as a writer if I was not saved by my disloyalty.... You remember the black and white squares of Bishop Blougram's chess board. As a novelist, I must be allowed to write from the point of view of the black square as well as of the white: doubt, even denial, must be given their chance of self-expression, or how is one freer than the Leningrad group?

But all this may be granted without abandoning the position outlined above, and the proof of this lies in Greene's own novels. For all the sordidness and vice which they describe, Greene's "Catholic" novels are so far from being "unedifying" that one critic, Angus Wilson, has felt justified in speaking[4] of "over-schematization", and others have seen them as practical exercises in theological casuistry (a con-

---

[3] In *Why do I Write? An Exchange of Views between Elizabeth Bowen, Graham Greene and V. S. Pritchett*, 1948.

[4] In *Evil and the Novelist Today*, a talk originally given in the Third Programme of the B.B.C. and published in the *Listener* of January 17th, 1963.

clusion which is lent some colour by the very title of the most recent, *A Burnt-out Case*, 1961).

In spite of the skill and sensitivity with which the West African background to *The Heart of the Matter* (1948) is painted one sometimes feels that Scobie's character and actions are being pushed and pulled in various not very likely directions in order to arrange a demonstration of pity carried to the *n*th degree, and to pose again more deliberately the question of last-second repentance and forgiveness already adumbrated in *Brighton Rock* (Pinkie says to Rose—rather surprisingly; it hardly seems in character—"You know what they say—'Between the stirrup and the ground, he something sought and something found.'") Scobie's ability to pity everyone but himself is admirable and moving, but his decision to deprive both the women he loves of his presence seems irrational as well as unnecessary; he knows in his heart that Helen Rolt could get on without him. But, that said, *The Heart of the Matter* remains a fine novel that does indeed probe to the very core of Christianity. Greene himself now takes the view that it is over-plotted. He has said[5] that he "doesn't like the book much ... one wanted to draw a fairly simple portrait of a man who was corrupted by his sense of pity. But in the course of (the) book, perhaps because one was rusty, not having written for some years during the war, one began to overload the plot, and I felt the impulse given by the character was whittled away."

On the same occasion Greene said that it was always his wish "to produce a central figure who represents some idea of reasonable simplicity—a mythical figure if you like." He feels that the nearest he came to "hitting the mythical element" was in *The Power and the Glory* (1940), the story of a "whisky-priest" on the run in a Mexican state in which religion is proscribed and priests are outlawed. It grew out of a visit to Mexico in 1938 which is described in *The Law-*

[5] In a symposium with Frank Kermode and Muriel Spark broadcast on the B.B.C. Third Programme, and printed in the *Listener* of August 30th, 1962.

less Roads (1939). Many of the characters and incidents which Greene came across in Mexico re-appear in the novel, where, without losing any of their reality or vividness, they have been given symbolical significance. The half-breed whom Greene met in Yajalon, with his "curly sideburns and two yellow fangs at either end of his mouth" has become the Judas-like mestizo who finally betrays the hunted priest to the police; Doc Winter has become the dentist Tench, who embodies the decay and decadence of the state of Tabasco, if not of the world in general. The hunted priest himself, with all his imperfections, symbolizes the power of God's love in a world which will not be saved by the socialist Utopianism of the police Lieutenant who pursues and captures him. The Lieutenant is the priest's logical antithesis: "There are mystics who are said to have experienced God directly. He was a mystic, too, and what he had experienced was vacancy—a complete certainty in the existence of a dying, cooling world, of human beings who had evolved from animals for no purpose at all. He knew." There are all kinds of levels and subtleties in *The Power and the Glory* which there is no space to indicate here; but it can also be read simply as a realistic account of a chase, capture and execution, and therein lies its success as a novel. It is Greene's most comprehensive projection of his vision of a world in which good and evil are continually at war; for most of the time the war is a cold one, but in parts of Mexico in the late thirties it was a hot war.

The theme of *The End of the Affair* (1951) is "God as plot-maker or novelist". A novelist called Bendrix falls in love, during the war, with Sarah Miles, the wife of a very conventional civil servant. A flying-bomb falls on Bendrix's house, and Sarah sees him pinned under the door, with one arm sticking out. Though not a believer, she vows to God in an access of fear and love that if Bendrix lives she will give him up for ever. Bendrix does live (it is implied that this is in fact a miracle, although the incident is explicable in natural terms) and the rest of the book is occupied with

Bendrix's vain efforts to induce Sarah to return to him. His pursuit of her results in her catching a chill from which she dies when she is on the point of becoming a Catholic. Her death is followed by further miracles which convince Bendrix that God exists, but leave him temporarily hating him for taking away the woman he loves. The book ends with Bendrix praying: "O God, You've done enough, You've robbed me of enough, I'm too tired and old to learn to love, leave me alone for ever."

This bare outline gives no idea of the art with which the book is written. The story is told largely through flash-backs and Sarah's diary, which Bendrix manages to lay his hands on through the agency of a private detective whom he hires to watch Sarah. The elaborately casual air of the narrative is reminiscent of Ford Madox Ford's *The Good Soldier*, a book for which Greene has a great admiration. Most critics feel that the miracles in *The End of the Affair* weaken the effect of the book, and Greene himself accepts the criticism; he said in the symposium already mentioned: "I had intended a much longer last part of the book, after the woman had died, where there was to be a succession of coincidences, until the lover became maddened by (them). I found it very difficult to continue the book without the central figure (Sarah) and I foreshortened badly by introducing something which was not easily accountable for in natural terms." Nonetheless, *The End of the Affair* is an extremely interesting and readable novel.

In 1953 Greene turned for the first time to the theatre. *The Living Room* (1953) and *The Potting Shed* (1957) are both pieces in his grimmest key; *The Potting Shed* reintroduces the idea of a vow or pact with God, this time in a very curious form: a priest asks God to take away his faith in return for his nephew's life. *The Complaisant Lover* (1961) is in a much lighter vein: a dentist's wife discovers that love affairs can fall very far short of expectations, and that husbands are not always as dull as they seem. It is a polished and amusing play which stands alone so far among Greene's work in its acceptance of conventional normality as a real and even pleasant possibility. The novels have continued to deal with expatriate graduates in misery.

The Quiet American (1955) contains a very convincing picture—based, as usual with Greene, on personal observation—of the fighting between the French and the Communists in Indo-China; its theme is the Jamesian one of American innocence confused and baffled by the corruption and decadence of the Old World. The narrator, Fowler, gets rid of the idealistic American, Pyle, before he can do too much harm, but Fowler's motives are not unimpeachable, for Pyle has robbed him of his mistress. *Our Man in Havana* (1958) is an uneasy mixture of comedy and tragedy (it is labelled "entertainment") which does not come off completely, although it has some extremely amusing moments. In it recurs the almost obsessional figure of the man with a wife and daughter from either or both of whom he is separated either spiritually or physically (Tench, Scobie). In his latest novel, *A Burnt-out Case* (1961), Greene returns to Africa; the central figure is a disillusioned architect in search of peace of mind who meets something like a martyr's death when he is shot by a man with whose wife he has for once never been to bed. Although depressingly bitter in tone, the book is an admirably honest (and readable) treatment of the problem of loss of belief. It is notoriously dangerous to identify characters with their creators, but it is difficult to resist the feeling that there is a good deal of Greene himself in Querry.

If Greene's world is a rather dismal one, it is also a wider and more comprehensive one than that of any other Christian novelist writing in the last fifty years; and if he does not always succeed in obtaining a perfect fusion of idea and reality, myth and "felt experience", that in itself is a testimony to the seriousness with which he has constantly attempted to relate his conception of Christianity to the world about him. No issues are evaded in Greene's religion; the responsibility for all the unpleasant things that go on in the

world is planted so firmly on God that it is hardly surprising
that Greene often seems to be involved, like his character
Bendrix, in a personal feud with God. It would be hypocritical
to pretend that this is an incomprehensible attitude.

ANTONIA WHITE

Another novelist of the same generation as Greene and
Waugh who deserves at least a mention is Antonia White
(b. 1899); a sensitive study of convent life, *Frost in May*
(1933), gained her the distinction of having her name deleted
for a time from the list of old pupils of Roehampton Convent.
Frost in May was followed by *The Lost Traveller* (1950), *The
Sugar House* (1952) and a number of other novels which all
possess, within the limits of their fairly restricted scope, the
compulsive quality of experienced truth.

As for the next generation, the three names that stand
out at the moment are those of William Golding, Morris West
and Muriel Spark.

WILLIAM GOLDING

William Golding was born in Cornwall in 1911, served in
the Navy during the war (this is reflected in the setting of
Pincher Martin, 1956), and after it became a schoolmaster at
Bishop Wordsworth's School, Salisbury. Golding has written
a good deal of poetry, but his name first caught the public
eye when he published the novel *Lord of the Flies* in 1954.
This highly original book deals with the adventures of a
party of schoolboys marooned on a coral island after an
aeroplane crash. In these ideal surroundings their life should
be idyllic; and so it is until their own natures and desires
begin to darken the picture. Golding includes the old Adam
that Ballantyne left out of his *Coral Island*. In fact, this self-
contained community of apparent innocents repeats in a
compressed form the history of man from the Garden of
Eden to the present. The symbolism does not obtrude and

the story is told with horrifying vividness and realism; nevertheless, the exceptional nature of the setting makes it difficult to regard the book as anything but a fable. The same is true of *Pincher Martin* (1956), in which the self-contained community has been reduced to a single individual, a naval officer struggling to save his life on a rock in the Atlantic. Descriptions of Martin's efforts to preserve his life alternate with pictures of his past life; at the end we learn that he actually died quite early on, so that what we have witnessed is the assumption by Martin's soul of the form his selfish life had made inevitable; Martin in purgatory, in fact, for it is implied that God's love will yet find its way past the two great claws to which Martin seems to be reduced. Martin is "fallen man —fallen more than most". The involved nature of the writing makes *Pincher Martin*[6] an interesting experiment rather than a completely successful novel; much the same is true of Golding's other novels, *The Inheritors* (1955) and *Free Fall*[7] (1959), although some critics rate them very highly. He has also written a play, *The Brass Butterfly* (1958).

MORRIS WEST

Morris West (b. 1916) is an Australian. In 1957 he published *Children of the Sun*, a passionately sincere if rather spun-out account of the urchins of Naples and Father Borrelli's efforts to help them. His first serious novel (he has also written thrillers), *The Second Victory* (1958), was set in Austria just after the end of the war; it had its moments, but was spoilt by too facile a dénouement. The hero, a Catholic officer in the British Army with a wife in England, falls in love with an Austrian girl, and has his problem solved by the news that his wife has been killed in air-crash on the way to join him in Austria.

[6] It has been subjected to a lengthy analysis by Michael Quinn in the Autumn 1962 issue of the *Critical Quarterly*.

[7] There was an interesting study of this novel by I. Gregor and M. Kinkeade-Weekes in the *Twentieth Century* for February, 1960.

The Devil's Advocate (1959) marked a considerable advance. Set in Italy, which West knows well, it is concerned with the investigation into the claims to beatification of a Calabrian peasant shot in mysterious circumstances by the Partisans in 1944 and since venerated locally as a saint. We are given to understand that even the identity of this Giacomo Nerone is not clear, so that West is enabled to give his novel all the suspense of a detective story. On this serviceable framework, which of itself implies and provokes an investigation into the nature of sanctity, the author has hung a number of other themes which may be loosely termed "religious". The Promoter of the Faith or Devil's advocate is an English priest dying of cancer who feels that he has lost—if he ever had—the capacity to love his fellow-men; the Contessa in whose house he stays is tormented by unsatisfied passion; and the painter whose patron she has become is a homosexual. For good measure we are given thumbnail sketches of a Roman cardinal and a provincial bishop, and the author's views on what is wrong with the Church in Italy. On the whole, West handles this indigestible mixture with considerable skill and the reader is able to swallow it with pleasure and profit. The characterization is convincing; the weakest part of the book is the writing itself, which occasionally sinks to this kind of theatricality:

> Then, quite suddenly, the truth hit him like cold water in the face. This man too had a cross to bear. Bishop he might be, but there were still doubts to plague him and fears to harry him on the high peak of temptation. A rare compassion stirred in the dry heart of Blaise Meredith and he answered quietly: "Does it matter? I think it matters much." "Why, Monsignor?" The deep, wise eyes challenged him. "Because I think that you, like me, are afraid of the finger of God."

On this showing, West is poised between Graham Greene and the Ethel Mannin of *Late Have I Loved Thee* (1948). His most recent novel, *The Shoes of the Fisherman* (1962), envisages a Ukrainian as pope; knowledgeable, intelligent and highly readable, it shows the same predilection for thematic density as *The Devil's Advocate*. Every possible problem that can plague a pope is introduced; even Teilhard de Chardin is brought in, thinly disguised as a Jesuit scientist called Télémond.

MURIEL SPARK

Muriel Spark is a more relaxed writer with a highly original comic style and an exceptional ear for dialogue. She became a Catholic some years ago, but her religion makes relatively casual entrances and exits in her writing. The most frequently recurring theme in her novels and short stories is the irruption of the supernatural or merely strange into the everyday, whether in the form of disembodied voices on the telephone (*Memento Mori*, 1959; the title indicates what the voices say) or people like Dougal Douglas (*The Ballad of Peckham Rye*, 1960) and that diverting if dangerous preparatory school teacher, Miss Jean Brodie (*The Prime of Miss Jean Brodie*, 1961), eventually betrayed by one of her star pupils, who picks up Catholicism through sleeping with Miss Brodie's old flame and ends up as Sister Helena of the Transfiguration. There is a hint of Waugh in Muriel Spark's themes and style, but her characterization is sharper, more individual, less stylized. A Waugh-like short story is *The Black Madonna* in the collection called *The Go-away Bird* (1958): a childless couple kindly offer strictly intellectual hospitality to lonely expatriate negroes. There is an outbreak of miracles in the parish; the couple pray for a child, and the prayer is answered—with a black baby. When Needle, the heroine of *A Ghost Speaks in the Portobello Road*, is murdered and the discovery of the body is announced in the headline "Needle—Found in Haystack", we are reminded of the closing stages of Waugh's *Black Mischief*, in which Basil Seal says to Prudence, "You're a grand girl, Prudence, and I'd like to eat you"—and eventually does. In contrast to Graham Greene, Muriel Spark says that for her the plot, not the character, is the myth; she prefers to "stick to a plot" or "formal outline", and deliberately writes what she calls "minor novels". Minor they may be in that their scope is restricted, but they are extremely effective; Muriel Spark is a talented and prolific writer; in half-a-dozen years she has produced as many books without giving any sign of repeating herself.

CHRISTOPHER DAWSON

To turn in conclusion from fiction to history, Christopher Dawson (b. 1889), who became a Catholic in 1914, has devoted most of his attention to the relation between religion and culture; *The Making of Europe* (1928) aims at showing that the period between A.D. 400 and 1000, in which the Church played such an important rôle, laid the foundations of all future development in Europe. In Dawson's view, the Church is "the representative in a changing world of an unchanging spiritual order".

HERBERT BUTTERFIELD

More recently, Herbert Butterfield, then Professor of Modern History in the University of Cambridge, made a considerable impression with the Christian view of history —or historical view of Christianity—which he expounded in *Christianity and History* (1949), whose seven chapters were originally delivered as lectures at Cambridge in 1948.

Christianity [says Butterfield in his introduction] is an historical religion in a particularly technical sense that the term possesses—it presents us with religious doctrines which are at the same time historical events or historical interpretations. . . . The fact that Christianity comes down to us as an historical religion . . . is bound to provide certain bearings for the interpretation of the whole drama of human life on this earth, bound to affect for example any views or dim feelings that we may have concerning the scheme of things in time.

Butterfield's style is a trifle drab and academic, but what he has to say is of extreme interest; it is a change to find a Christian successfully playing Vico and Spengler at their own game.

CHAPTER II

AMERICA

The novel has flourished in America in the last thirty or
forty years—William Faulkner and James Gould Cozzens
have published work that is at least the equal of that produced anywhere in the world during the same period—but
the front rank of novelists does not include any expressly
Christian writers. There is Christian imagery in Faulkner
(the hero of *A Fable* is a sort of Christ in modern dress) and
Scott Fitzgerald (notably in the short story *The Diamond as
Big as the Ritz,* with its "village of Fish" and the "twelve
men" who are meant to remind us of the Apostles), and
Hemingway, like Fitzgerald, was born a Catholic, but none
of these novelists writes as a Christian. On the other hand,
the most decidedly Christian historical novels of writers
like Louis de Wohl and Lloyd C. Douglas (*The Robe,* 1942;
The Big Fisherman, 1948), can hardly be regarded as important pieces of creative literature.

WILLA CATHER

For a novelist of the first rank who writes sympathetically
of Christian themes we must go back to Willa Cather (1876–
1947), the chronicler of the western frontier, who ended her
days as an Episcopalian. Christianity, or to be precise, the
Catholic Church and its representatives, is given a prominent
rôle in the two historical novels *Death Comes for the Archbishop* (1927) and *Shadows on the Rock* (1931). *Death
Comes for the Archbishop,* perhaps Willa Cather's best

novel, is an apparently simple but impressive tale of the
work of two French Catholic missionaries in New Mexico
in the nineteenth century. The episodic construction results
in a certain lack of tension, but this is deliberate; the author
herself once described the texture of *Shadows on the Rock*
as "mainly anacoluthon".

In an essay on the *Archbishop,* she said that she had long
been tantalized by the possibility of imitating a pictorial
model in prose. Since she had first seen the Puvis de Cha-
vannes frescoes of the life of St Geneviève she had wanted
to write "something without accent, with none of the artificial
elements of composition". She wanted to show how all human
experiences, whether noble or trivial, spring from "one
supreme spiritual experience". "The essence of such writing,"
she said, "is not to hold the note, not to use an incident for
all there is in it—but to touch and pass on." The limpid and
quietly told story of the efforts of Frs Latour and Vaillant
(the two central characters were based on two real priests,
Archbishop Lang and Fr. Machebeuf) to spread and strengthen
Christianity in the south-west of the United States, efforts
which bring them into collision with degenerate Spanish
priests and Indian superstitions, is thus a good deal more
subtle than it seems at first sight. Like all Willa Cather's
frontier novels, *Death Comes for the Archbishop* is an
allegory of the individual's devotion to an overriding spiritual
purpose in the face of the cold realities of everyday life. The
following extract will give some idea of the quality of the
writing and the general atmosphere of the novel (Fr Vaillant
is talking):

> Down near Tucson a Pima Indian convert once asked me
> to go off into the desert with him, as he had something to
> show me. He took me into a place so wild that a man less
> accustomed to these things might have mistrusted and feared
> for his life. We descended into a terrifying canyon of black
> rock, and there in the depths of a cave, he showed me a golden
> chalice, vestments and cruets, all the paraphernalia for cele-
> brating Mass. His ancestors had hidden these sacred objects

there when the mission was sacked by Apaches, he did not know how many generations ago. The secret had been handed down in his family, and I was the first priest who had ever come to restore to God his own. To me, that is the situation in a parable. The Faith in that wild frontier is like a buried treasure; they guard it, but they do not know how to use it to their soul's salvation. A word, a prayer, a service, is all that is needed to set free those souls in bondage. I confess I am covetous of that mission. I desire to be the man who restores these lost children to God. It will be the greatest happiness of my life.

Though not a Catholic herself, Willa Cather penetrates wonderfully into the characters of her two priests, the intellectual Latour and the more earthily practical Vaillant, and there can be no doubt that she is very much in sympathy with the ideas which they represent. *Death Comes for the Archbishop* is a sort of Christian legend which brings home powerfully the timeless continuity of religious faith, however various the forms it may assume in different peoples and different ages. *Shadows on the Rock* is another variation on the same theme; set in Quebec towards the end of the seventeenth century, it paints a serene but vivid picture of French Canada and the tradesmen, priests and governors who gave it its solid strength.

HENRY MORTON ROBINSON

Henry Morton Robinson (b. 1898) is a writer of a very different kind: extremely skilful and professional, but far less profound. Although he is, and always has been, a Roman Catholic, only one of his novels, *The Cardinal* (1950), reflects the fact; there is nothing religious about *The Big Snow* (1947). Robinson has said himself: "I shall probably never write about the Catholic Church again. . . . I am not a propagandist or a proselytizer—but merely a writer. My vocation is not with the *Word* but with words." Although, as we suggested earlier, the Christian must regard literature as something ultimately smaller than his religion, he does not expect the novelist to be simply a propagandist or a proselytizer. Nevertheless, like everyone else, he does expect consistency of outlook in a serious writer, and its absence in Robinson is surprising and disappointing. For all that, *The Cardinal,* judged in itself, is an extremely effective novel; once picked up, it is difficult to put down. It traces the career of a priest called Stephen Fermoyle, born of Irish parents in Robinson's own city of Boston, from his ordination to his elevation to the cardinalate. Many of the outward events in Fermoyle's life correspond to details in the career of Cardinal Spellman (who, by the way, has himself written a novel: *The Foundling,* 1951); but essentially he is a fictional creation of the author.

"As a writer," Robinson says in the preface, "I was struck long ago by wonder and awe at the Priest's function. In *The Cardinal* I have attempted to express these feelings by describing a gifted but very human priest fulfilling his destiny as a consecrated mediator between God and man." The chief criticism which both the book and its central character provoke is that they are larger and simpler than life. Everything that could possibly happen to an American priest does happen to Stephen Fermoyle, including capture by the Ku Klux Klan, and he meets it all with rather too much aplomb. Similarly, the divine pattern in the world is traced with too much facility. As a young man, Stephen has to choose between the life of his younger sister, Mona, and that of her unborn child (it is too late for a Caesarean operation); he makes the correct choice, and is rewarded many years later, as a cardinal in Rome, when he watches his young niece playing the piano at a big society gathering:

> Happiness, differing in kind and intensity from any he had yet known, filled Stephen as he watched Regina at the piano. This was Mona's daughter, more beautiful, more gifted than Mona—a soul obviously at ease before perfection, capable of loving and growing in its light. This was the child the white-coated doctor would have destroyed in routine fashion. In eighteen short years, the centre of God's circle had been re-

vealed. From the broken arc of Mona's life, He had shaped
this perfect round.

The Cardinal is an extremely talented, entertaining and sometimes (though not in the passage quoted) moving performance,
but it is not great literature.

THOMAS MERTON

Nor is *Seven Storey Mountain* (1948; published in England
under the title *Elected Silence*), the autobiography of Thomas
Merton, who in 1941 entered the Cistercian monastery of
Gethsemani in Kentucky and has since produced a highly
successful series of books which must be regarded as devotional in nature and hence outside the terms of reference of
this survey. However, if it is not quite great literature, *Seven
Storey Mountain* is nevertheless a compelling and honest,
though sometimes over-emotional, account of a young man's
search for spiritual satisfaction. Moreover, it has a certain
universal significance in that the experiences which it describes typify (except for the Trappist vocation) those of
many young men of Merton's generation, confused as they
were not only by the lack of any solid moral or religious
basis on which to live their lives but also by the alarms and
excursions of a Europe already on the march to war. Merton's father was a painter from New Zealand; his mother was
an American. His parents were often on the move from
country to country, from continent to continent (to this extent,
of course, Merton's experiences are not typical), and this
peripatetic bohemian existence led, as it often does, to an
unnatural and aimless intellectual precocity. Merton eventually went to Oakham School and then on to Cambridge,
(by this time his parents were dead and he was in the care
of a guardian), but he wasted his time at Cambridge and
never completed his course. It was decided that he should go
back to his relations in America. There he graduated at
Columbia University, and went on to teach at St Bona-

venture's, a Franciscan college in New York State. By this
time he was a Catholic and thinking seriously of the priesthood. After one or two false starts, he found his spiritual
home with the Trappists of Gethsemani, and there he has
been ever since, condemned to physical silence but producing
on his typewriter a certain amount of poetry and a succession
of distinguished meditations on the spiritual and moral problems of this—and every—age.

JOHN HOWARD GRIFFIN

A book that has certain distant affinities with *Seven Storey
Mountain* is the novel *The Devil Rides Outside* (1953) by
the young Texan Catholic, John Howard Griffin, who was
blinded in the Second World War but has since recovered
his sight. It is a twopence, highly-coloured account of the
struggle between spirit and flesh. A young, unnamed American student (the story is told in the first person and partly
in diary form), who apparently feels some kind of urge towards the religious life, has left Paris and his girl-friend to
do research in a monastery in the French countryside. He
finds the rigours of monastic life too much and goes to live
in the village outside the monastery gates; but there he discovers that the real enemy is within himself, and after an
extraordinary love-hate relationship with the middle-aged
woman in whose house he takes his meals—and other
amorous adventures—he returns to his cell in the monastery.
The Devil Rides Outside made a considerable impact on
intelligent critics when it was first published. It is an extraordinary book; rather the raw material of a novel than the
novel itself; like other American novels published since the
war, it makes a virtue of suppressing absolutely nothing. The
paper-back edition was banned in Detroit by a Catholic
censorship organization. The style is deliberately unpolished
and relies heavily on the historic present; from time to time

the stream-of-consciousness technique is employed. The following extract is a typical sample:

9 December

Sombre days again. Days without sun. The snows of a month have become the frozen filth of many footprints, reddened in the courtyard by gravel sprinkled there to keep us from falling.

Since Matins the morning has been spent working out a problem in morality, given us by Father Clément in his spiritual conference last evening. It is concerned with whether the renunciation of spiritual riches is a legitimate part of the vow of poverty. In some of the severer orders, tastes in music and art and literature are eschewed by the monks, who feel that their vows of poverty are not complete unless they include poverty of the spirit as well as of physical considerations. It contradicts the parable of talents. I arrive at no solution, hoping I won't be called upon in class to-day.

The cold becomes unbearable and I take my work to bed with me. The bed warms. Words imperceptibly detach themselves from the page. Words pulse in consciousness of eye near the page. Walls sweat. Wetness dribbles from steamed walls. Is a vow of poverty, does a vow of poverty legitimately include poverty of spiritual riches? The words focus into warmth beneath covering blanket. Move deeper into the bed. Poverty and richness of spiritual riches. The room turns. Dark outside the window of morning. Sweat on walls running down. Breaking away and running down. Hermetic rigidness and a tightening of smells. Smells and a tiny square of bareness on covered flesh. A coughing. Wheezing. Swallowing. Snorting. Head returns to its pillow. Back to the other. No class. In poverty there is. Walls dark with shadowed crucifix. Walls near bed. Turning from walls. Grit and musk and floor of mould. Pornography of. Sanctity in. Poverty. Back, back. The return. Footsteps in the hall. Approaching. There. Fading. Heavier breathing of rattling palate. Back. And back is return and behind. Either one. Back is return to questions. Of poverty. And ass. Either one. Black-robed nun with skirts and kindness of face. Kindness of all in poverty. Aching at nape. On and on and off to the other. Smell of bareness. It draws near and. It recedes. Kaleidoscope. Back is poverty. Legitimate. Night of all nativities. Phantasmagoria of back. On and on ..." (pp. 79–80).

And on, for 443 closely-printed pages; but clearly Griffin is a writer of tremendous vitality. His second novel, *Nuni* (1956), is similar in theme to Golding's *Lord of the Flies*. A professor of English is the sole survivor of an aeroplane crash on a South Sea island, where he comes into contact with a primitive, taboo-ridden society which seems to symbolize human evil in general, and possibly modern American society in particular.

J. F. POWERS

J. F. Powers (b. 1917, in Jacksonville, Illinois) is at the opposite pole to Griffin both in style and content. His urbane and witty stories of the daily trials of Catholic priests are reminiscent less of Hemingway or Mailer than of the *New Yorker,* in which indeed many of them first appeared. Powers says that he writes about priests "because they are engaged in the only race worth running ... and their failures and successes are, therefore, more truly stories". One or two of the short stories in the collections *Prince of Darkness* (1947) and *The Presence of Grace* (1956) might be held to justify this somewhat portentous utterance, but most of them deal with the marginalia of clerical life. The narrator in some of the most amusing is Fritz, Pastor Malt's black cat, who, in his daily struggle to make sure that he gets the best of everything, proves himself a shrewd observer of curates. But for all their lightness of touch, Powers's stories often provide a biting commentary on the less edifying aspects of American Catholic life (and, of course, *mutatis mutandis,* Catholic life in other countries, too). *The Devil Was the Joker* describes the activities of a man who peddles the magazine and pamphlets of a down-at-heel religious Order (and much else besides, on his own account) round the parishes of the Middle West. One of the items in his bag is a new kind of rosary:

It was made of plastic, to fit the hand, and in function and appearance it was similar to an umpire's ball-and-strike indicator. Each time a little key was punched, the single dial, which showed the mysteries—Sorrowful, Joyful and Glorious —revolved a notch, and for the Ave Marias there was a modest tick, for the Pater Nosters an authoritative click. Mac had difficulty explaining the new rosary's purpose to some priests —*not* to replace the old model, the traditional beads on a string; but to facilitate prayer while driving, for the new rosary was easily attached to the steering wheel. "Of course, you still have to say the prayers," Mac would say.

There is room in every age for a writer like Powers; he has the gift of amusing and destroying without any suggestion of a sneer. His talent is seen to its best advantage in the short story; his novel, *Morte d'Urban* (1962) leaves one with the impression that the material has been stretched rather further than it will comfortably go.

MARY GILBERT

The short stories of Sister Mary Gilbert, SNJM (Madeline de Frees), who teaches at Holy Names College, Spokane, are broadly similar in content to those of Powers, but considerably gentler and less incisive in tone. *The Model Chapel,* which gained a place in *The Best American Short Stories of 1962,* is a polished and amusing but superficial vignette of convent life. Sister Mary Gilbert also writes poetry. In 1953 she published an autobiographical account of convent life called *Springs of Silence.*

MARY McCARTHY

It is a commonplace that some of the most convincing writing about Catholicism has been produced by writers who subsequently left the Church. For a vivid picture of Irish Catholicism and Jesuit schools, where would one go but to James Joyce?[1] A similar case in America is that of Mary

[1] This aspect of Joyce has been studied by J. Mitchell Morse in *The Sympathetic Alien: James Joyce and Catholicism*, London, Peter Owen and Vision Press, 1959. Morse prefaces his book with a quotation from *Finnegan's Wake*: "The ring man in the rong shop but the rite words by the rote order!"

McCarthy. Her *Memories of a Catholic Girlhood* (1957) contain, among other things, a vivid and by no means unsympathetic picture of life in a Sacred Heart convent in Seattle, a picture that forms a sort of transatlantic pendant to Antonia White's *Frost in May*. However, when Miss McCarthy turns to criticism of Catholicism, her generalizations tend to be a trifle wild.

> From what I have seen, I am driven to the conclusion that religion is only good for good people, and I do not mean this as a paradox, but simply as an observable fact. Only good people can afford to be religious. For the others, it is too great a temptation—a temptation to the deadly sins of pride and anger, chiefly, but one might also add sloth. My Grandmother McCarthy, I am sure, would have been a better woman if she had been an atheist or an agnostic. The Catholic religion, I believe, is the most dangerous of all, morally (I do not know about the Moslem), because, with its claim to be the only true religion, it fosters that sense of privilege I spoke of earlier —the notion that not everyone is lucky enough to be a Catholic.

This "sense of privilege" is doubtless to be found occasionally in unthinking Catholics, but Miss McCarthy must know perfectly well that there is not the slightest justification for it in Catholic teaching.

ALLEN TATE AND CAROLINE GORDON

Christianity in general—and Catholicism in particular—is an important force in contemporary American intellectual life. The poets it has influenced or produced, such as Robert Lowell and the Dominican William Everson, lie outside the scope of this book, but several other prose-writers besides those already mentioned have published work of distinction in the last twenty or thirty years. The most interesting are the critic Allen Tate and his wife, Caroline Gordon (b. 1895), who writes novels and short stories, and the novelists Claude Koch and Flannery O'Connor. Allen Tate (b. 1899), who is also a poet with a considerable reputation and the author of an extremely good novel about the Civil War (*The Fathers,* 1938), is Professor of English at the University of Minnesota. He and his wife became Catholics some fifteen years ago. His criticism was always, as it were, potentially Christian in tone and one of his latest collections, *The Forlorn Demon* (1952), reflects, like Caroline Gordon's later novels, (for example *The Strange Children,* 1951), the influence of Maritain. He is a Southerner, born in Clarke County, Kentucky, and through him Catholic influence on Southern literature— including Faulkner—has been considerable. The Agrarian movement which he helped to found in the thirties, with Robert Penn Warren and others, is reminiscent of the ideas of men like Péguy, Belloc and Chesterton. Though conceived as a defence of the old rural economy of the Southern States as opposed to the urban values of the North, it was fundamentally a plea for a more organic society. Tate himself has put it like this:

> I never thought of Agrarianism as a restoration of anything in the Old South; I saw it as something to be created, as I think it will in the long run be created as the result of a profound change, not only in the South, but elsewhere, in the moral and religious outlook of Western man. . . . What I had in mind twenty years ago, not too clearly, I think I see more clearly now, that is, the possibility of the humane life presupposes with us, a moral order, the order of a unified Christendom. . . .

Like Waugh, Tate regards technology without Christianity as "barbarism quite simply, but barbarism refined, violent, and decadent, not the vigorous barbarism of the forest and the soil".

FLANNERY O'CONNOR

Flannery O'Connor (b. 1925) too, is a Southerner, from Georgia. Her work reflects a fierce, medieval sort of Catholicism which has something in common with the hell-fire, prophetic Baptist Christianity that is the dominant form of religion in the South, where Catholics form only about three per cent of the population. This revivalist Christianity makes frequent appearances in the collection of brutally direct short stories by Flannery O'Connor entitled *A Good Man Is Hard to Find* (1955) and sets the tone of her excellent novel, *The Violent Bear It Away* (1955; British ed., 1960), which is a profound and subtle study of the way in which God impinges on man. A boy of fourteen, brought up in the backwoods of Tennessee by a pious old great-uncle, attempts to reject the mission of prophecy handed down to him by the old man. He drowns a dim-witted child—his cousin—in a desperate attempt to exorcize the memory of his great-uncle, but even as he does so he involuntarily utters the formula of baptism over the drowning child. The theme of the book is driven home in its imagery: for instance, the materialist Rayber's unplugging of his hearing aid to disconnect himself from those aspects of reality which he is determined to ignore; and the boy's insatiable hunger, which is finally revealed as hunger for the bread of life and is described at the climax of the story, when the boy at last recognizes and accepts his vocation, in this striking passage:

> He felt his hunger no longer as a pain but as a tide. He felt it rising in himself through time and darkness, rising through the centuries, and he knew that it rose in a line of men whose lives were chosen to sustain it, who would wander in the world, strangers from that violent country where the silence is never broken except to shout the truth.

Flannery O'Connor's observation of character is precise, her dialogue natural and her language vivid, earthy and economical. *The Violent Bear it Away* is one of those rare novels that make the reader feel that they had to be written, and could have been written in no other way.

CLAUDE KOCH

Claude Koch (b. 1918) is a Northerner from Philadelphia. His novel *Light in Silence* (1958) recalls in its setting—the

College of the Order of St Bardolph—the work of J. F. Powers, but the tone is very different: lyrical and diffuse rather than crisp and ironical. One of the brothers, Finian Joseph, loses faith in the work of the order and decides that he must return to the world; he finds that it is a wrong decision, and that "there is no wisdom except in submission".

It is perhaps worth ending this chapter with a reminder that a concern with Christianity can be traced in many contemporary American writers who are not in fact practising Christians. We have already mentioned the case of Faulkner; a more recent one is that of another Southern novelist, William Styron, who sees the modern American as a sort of hollow man obsessed with death and damnation. The wife of the hero of *Set This House on Fire* (1959; British ed., 1961) is a Catholic, and seems to represent life as opposed to death and emptiness in this somewhat lurid novel set in Italy. America is in a state of transition; it is not altogether surprising that many of the writers who have questioned the premises of the American way of life should show a particular interest in a system of values which takes account of deeper layers of thought and feeling.

CHAPTER III

FRANCE

If we leave aside Léon Bloy and Charles Péguy—both dead by 1917 and discussed in an earlier volume in this series—Christian writing in France in the last fifty years is dominated by the figures of Claudel, Bernanos, Mauriac and Julien Green. Of these, the most striking—and perhaps the greatest—is Claudel; but before we consider him, it will be as well to set the scene by taking a quick look at some lesser writers of his own or the preceding generation.

PAUL BOURGET

Paul Bourget (1852–1935) began his literary career by publishing some volumes of neo-romantic verse, but soon turned to the novel; *Le Disciple* (1889) was important in that it marked the beginning of the reaction from Zolaesque naturalism back to the classical psychological novel. Roughly speaking, *Le Disciple* and the long series of extremely competent novels that followed it deal with the moral problems of the upper middle classes; they have been compared with those of Henry James, but do not reflect the same convoluted subtlety. Their interest for us lies in the fact that they are written from a Catholic point of view; Bourget described them as exercises in "apologétique expérimentale", which consisted, he said, in establishing that "étant donné une série d'observations sur la vie humaine, tout dans ces observations

s'est passé comme si le Christianisme était vrai."[1] This may
be accepted as a perfect description of the ideal Christian
novel (if such a thing could exist). Unfortunately, Bourget's
practice does not measure up to his theory. A story can
illustrate an idea, but it cannot establish its validity; Bourget
proceeds from the idea to the characters, instead of from
the characters to the ideas. *L'Etape* (1903), *Un Divorce* (1904),
L'Emigré (1907) and *Le Démon de Midi* (1914) are all
romans à thèse. *L'Etape* is supposed to demonstrate that,
given two families, the one that has risen too swiftly from
the peasant to the professional classes is bound to end up
in immorality and misery, while the old-fashioned one that
sticks to its Catholic traditions will find peace and happiness.
Obviously, the reverse could equally well happen; the "new"
family might be vigorous and virtuous, the "old" one tired
and decadent. As a contemporary critic, Jacques Rivière,
put it (he himself returned to Catholicism under the influence
of Claudel; the letters they exchanged between 1902 and
1914 were published in 1926): "(Bourget's) characters are not
living beings; they are hospital patients, laboratory props,
anatomical specimens on which the professor carries out his
demonstration."

The name of Jacques Rivière (1886–1925) recalls that of
another critic of this period who eventually became a Catholic, Charles du Bos (1882–1939). A graduate of Balliol College, Oxford, Du Bos was partly of American ancestry, and
his speciality was the interpretation of foreign thought and
literature; his *Journal* (1955) contains many comments on
English literature and English writers. The essays entitled
Du spirituel dans l'ordre littéraire (1955) reflects his interest
in philosophy and religion. He was received into the Catholic
Church in 1927, and one of his last books dealt with the
problems of the Catholic novelist (*François Mauriac et le
problème du romancier catholique,* 1933).

[1] "Given a series of observations of human life, everything observed
has happened as if Christianity were true."

ERNEST PSICHARI

Bourget was a monarchist as well as a Catholic; he was one of the founder-members of the traditionalist reaction against the socialism and materialism of the end of the nineteenth century. Politically, this movement ended in the excesses of the *Action Française,* denounced in 1926 by Cardinal Andrieu of Bordeaux as a hot-bed of "atheism, agnosticism, anti-Christianism, anti-Catholicism, amoralism and paganism". An earlier and more admirable side of the movement was the wave of patriotic and religious fervour just before the First World War which produced writers like Charles Péguy and Ernest Psichari (1883–1914), both of whom were killed in the first year of the war. Psichari, who was brought up as an unbeliever and gradually came to accept Christianity when he was serving as an officer in North Africa, may be regarded as symbolizing the revolt against nineteenth-century agnosticism, for he was a grandson of Renan. Curiously enough, Claudel, too, had a direct contact with Renan; when Claudel was still a school-boy at the Lycée Louis-le-Grand in Paris, Renan came to distribute the prizes, and in his speech he told the assembled students that it might be that some day one of them would denounce him as a corrupter of youth. The prophecy was amply fulfilled; Claudel never ceased to denounce him later on. A choice example occurs in one of Claudel's later books, the Biblical study entitled *Paul Claudel interroge l'apocalypse* (1946), where, with that confident, not to say rude, intolerance which was one of his less likable characteristics, he speaks of Renan as "le plus visqueux des batraciens . . . Non seulement, il croit à la boue et à quelque chose de plus confortable encore et de plus mollet que le néant, qui est le doute, mais il l'aime, il s'y vautre avec délices."[2]

---

[2] "The slimiest of the batrachians. . . . . Not only does he believe in the mud and in something still more comfortable and softer than a vacuum, namely, doubt, but he likes it, he enjoys rolling in it."

Psichari described the process of his conversion in the auto-biographical novel, *Le Voyage du Centurion* (The Centurion's Journey) (1915). The term "novel" is really misleading (in French the untranslatable term "récit" would be employed), for the book is hardly more than one long meditation by the hero, Maxence, as he leads his troops on their various military and administrative tasks through the sands and oases of Mauretania. Maxence is an *anima naturaliter christiana* who has had the misfortune to be borne "fils d'un colonel lettré, voltairien et pis". He wants to believe, but because there is a Montaigne in him as well as a Pascal (as there is in most Frenchmen) he must be able to justify his faith by reason. But Maxence does eventually find his way to God, and we leave him on his knees saying his first *Our Father*. The "centurion" of the book's title is the centurion of the Gospel, and one of the key ideas of *Le Voyage du centurion* is the parallel between the grandeur and servitude of the soldier and the grandeur and the servitude of the Christian. Another is the special position of France in Christendom.

Patriotism and devotion to Christ thus merge into the same thing; especially in face of the Moslem Moors. Although a trifle monotonous in tone, the book is impressive in its sincerity and simplicity (the simplicity is the product of art, not spontaneity; there was a first, directly autobiographical draft, suppressed by Psichari but published six years after his death under the title *Les Voix qui crient dans le désert*); it is written in a lucid but rhapsodic French that defies translation. There is one observation in it which, though in a sense a commonplace, prefigures curiously the theme of Bruce Marshall's *Father Malachy's Miracle*: "There are men who claim to love the truth. But if a truth comes from God, they reject it and veil their faces like hypocrites and pharisees. . . . Even if they saw the dead rise again at Lourdes, and the halt walk straight, they would still say 'No', in their devilish malice."

PAUL CLAUDEL

And so we come to Paul Claudel (1868–1955). Claudel was primarily a poet and dramatist, but it would be unthinkable not to mention him in a survey of modern Christian literature, even one which is mainly concerned with prose. Although he spent much of his life abroad—he was a career diplomat who served all over the world, finishing up as French Ambassador in Brussels—and although some of his most important plays were not staged until the 'forties, Claudel made his presence strongly felt in French literature throughout the first half of the century. Among the writers he converted or re-converted to Catholicism were the critic Jacques Rivière and the poet Francis Jammes, and for twenty-five years he battled by letter to win over André Gide as well.

Claudel came of a Catholic, but not particularly pious, family in the Tardenois; his own real conversion dated from a moment at Vespers in Notre-Dame on Christmas Day 1886, when he experienced a sudden spiritual awakening. Earlier in the same year he had made the acquaintance of the *Illuminations* of Rimbaud, who gave him, he said, "la révélation du surnaturel", so that if it were necessary to sum up Claudel's work in one brief phrase, the phrase would be "Christian symbolism". However, such a description would be quite inadequate, for Claudel's poetry and plays are like nothing before or since in French literature. They reflect wide reading in most of the world's literature, they rest on a carefully thought out philosophical or theological basis, and they are dominated by the wish, not only to interpret the universe in a Christian sense, but to bring home the truth of this interpretation to the reader or spectator. Claudel wrote in a letter to Rivière, "art is only a pale counterfeit of holiness", and he is reported by Gide as saying at a meeting between the two in 1905:

I attach absolutely no value to the literary quality of my work. Frizeau [a friend of Francis Jammes and Jacques

Rivière] was the first one who, brought back to God by my dramas, because he saw religion dominating everything in them, made me think: then I haven't written in vain. The literary beauty of my work has no other significance for me than that found by a workman who is aware of having performed his task well; I simply did my best; but had I been a carpenter, I should have been just as conscientious in planing a plank properly as I have been in writing properly.

(André Gide, *Journal*, trans. John Russell, London, 1952.)

The artist himself is not always in the best position to judge his own work, but these remarks are interesting because they indicate that, on a conscious level at least, Claudel subscribed to the view of literature outlined in the introduction to this book.

I deliberately used the word "universe" just now in speaking of Claudel's work, for one of its most striking characteristics is the attempt to present God, man and world as a totality. In his *Traité de la Connaissance*, Claudel defines the poet, and indeed man in general, as the one whose job it is to "re-present" the creation of the Creator: "Tout passe, et, rien n'étant présent, tout doit être représenté." Man is a sort of microcosm of the world: "Il est des choses l'image comprenante, et consommante, l'hostie intelligible en qui elles sont consommées."

The breadth of Claudel's conceptions are reflected in the scope of his most important play, *Le Soulier de Satin* (1928–9), which was translated into English in 1931 by Chesterton's Father Brown, Monsignor John O'Connor. The action of *The Satin Slipper* covers nearly a century, from 1545 to 1640, and stretches over three continents; it is a sort of cosmic drama that has more in common with the baroque plays of Calderon than with anything in French literature. There are four long acts and a huge number of characters. The theme is the guilty love of Don Rodrigue and Doña Prouhèze, which is spiritualized by separation and renunciation. The title refers to the slipper which Doña Prouhèze puts in the hand of a statue of the Virgin, so that when she is tempted to

rush headlong into evil, she will limp. God reaches Don Rodrigue and Doña Prouhèze through their suffering, for suffering
is a necessary stage in redemption, and indeed, as Prouhèze's
guardian angel tells her, "Even sin! Sin, too, can be of service". *The Satin Slipper* is both a Catholic and a catholic play;
it is undoubtedly one of the masterpieces of the last fifty years.

When he retired from the French Foreign Service in 1935,
Claudel went to live at Brangues in eastern France, and
there, during the last twenty years of his life, he produced
a series of prose meditations on Scripture: *Introduction au
livre de Ruth* (1938); *Un poète regarde la Croix* (1938); *Paul
Claudel interroge l'Apocalypse* (1946); *Le Livre de Job*
(1946); *Paul Claudel interroge le Cantique des Cantiques*
(1948); and *Emmäus* (1949). For the most part, these books
are symbolical and analogical interpretations of Scripture,
interspersed with vitriolic comments on people and things of
which Claudel disapproved. He was one of those men who,
once having made up their mind about a thing, never again
waver in their opinion about it, and his devotion to the
Church was complete. But authoritarian and dogmatic though
he was by nature, he was not narrow-minded or uncharitable.
Although he was horrified by Gide's avowal of his homosexual inclinations, Claudel wrote back on March 9th, 1914:

> My poor Gide, I should not have written to you if I were
> not still your friend. I admit that that passage in the N.R.F.
> [the homosexual dream in *Les Caves du Vatican*] came to me
> as a shock! But I'm too old a hand to be scandalized by any-
> thing, and I don't really know what right I should have to
> judge anybody.

The whole correspondence between Claudel and Gide,
published in France in 1949 and in England (translated by
John Russell) in 1952, is of absorbing interest, because it is
a debate between the two sides of the French mind, indeed
of the human mind. Claudel plays Pascal or Bossuet to
Gide's Montaigne or Voltaire; Claudel's answer to any given
question is "yes" or "no", Gide's is usually "yes and no". Had

Claudel convinced Gide, Gide's later books would obviously have been very different; but there was never any real danger that Gide would yield. His Protestant upbringing and his determination to achieve, as Goethe tried to, some kind of ideal of "humanity" independent of God combined to prevent him from ever feeling able to accept a solution guaranteed by authority.

One last word about Claudel: he did not publish a voluminous *Journal*, like Gide, or write an autobiography, but during 1951 and 1952 he did give a series of forty-two interviews on the French radio to Jean Amrouche, and these were subsequently published, in 1954, as *Mémoires improvisées* (*Improvised Memoirs*). They make a fascinating commentary on Claudel's life and work.

GEORGES BERNANOS

Of the three considerable Christian novelists of twentieth-century France—Bernanos, Mauriac and Green—the oldest is Mauriac. However, it will be appropriate to discuss Georges Bernanos (1888–1948) first, for apart from the fact that he has already been dead for some fifteen years his work shows some affinities with that of Claudel. Like Claudel's, Bernanos' work is most decidedly Catholic, and like Claudel Bernanos has no use for the sceptic: in his very first novel an un-flattering portrait of Anatole France is introduced, and in his last, the curiously confused *Monsieur Ouine* (1946), the villain of the piece is Monsieur Ouine himself, a consumptive teacher of languages whose very name is apparently meant to indicate that he is a man who has said "oui au néant" ("yes to the void"). Bernanos' world is a lurid one in which one priest meets the devil face to face and another is murdered and impersonated by a Lesbian, but there is no denying the penetration of his psychological insight or the sincerity and strength of his Christianity, and of all the writers of fiction we have so far considered he most deserves the description "Catholic novelist."

Bernanos was born in Paris and spent his childhood in the Pas de Calais, a region which provides the background to many of his novels. He was educated at the Jesuit Collège de Vaugirard in Paris, where he knew Charles and Xavier de Gaulle. As a student, he joined the *Action Française,* and at one point was imprisoned after being arrested in a demonstration. He became a journalist, and by 1913 was editor of a monarchist weekly at Rouen, *L'Avant-Garde de Normandie.* During the First World War he served as a corporal with the Sixth Dragoons, fought on the Somme and at Verdun, and was wounded several times. After the war he took a job with an insurance company in order to support his family (he had married in 1917), but tried to write in his spare moments. The period of convalescence after a serious illness gave him time to finish his first novel, *Sous le Soleil de Satan,* which was read with enthusiasm by Robert Vallery-Radot, the editor of the review *L'Univers,* and published by Plon on the advice of the philosopher Jacques Maritain. The success of this book enabled, or at any rate encouraged, Bernanos to devote all his time to writing. From then onwards he led a pretty nomadic life, although an accident on his motor-cycle in 1933 made a permanent cripple of him. Lack of money drove him for a time to the Balearic Islands, and the Munich agreement to Brazil, where he remained until the end of the war. In 1945 he returned to France, and in 1947 moved on to Tunisia. He died in Paris of a liver complaint in 1948.

Sous le Soleil de Satan (Eng. tr., *The Star of Satan*) (1926) falls into two quite distinct sections. The first part, *L'Histoire de Mouchette,* is superficially like a Victorian novelette. Mouchette is Germaine Malorthy, sixteen-year-old daughter of a rich miller in the Boulogne district. She has been having an affair with the local medical officer of health, Gallet, who is also a Socialist Member of Parliament. She is now expecting a child, and in a hysterical frame of mind she goes to the local squire, the Marquis de Cadignan, accuses him of being the father of the child, and shoots him, in such a way that

the crime is taken for suicide. Cadignan is thus saddled with
the responsibility for the child, and Gallet and Mouchette
share a guilty secret. This sordid little story takes only eighty-
odd pages to tell, but it is given a spiritual depth that makes
it more reminiscent of Dostoevsky than of Zola or Mau-
passant.

The second and longer half of *The Star of Satan* starts off
on an apparently quite different tack. We are introduced to
Abbé Donissan, who has just arrived as curate to the aristocratic and fastidious Canon Menou-Segrais (priests play an
important part in many of Bernanos' novels). Donissan is a
rough country lad who gets on Menou-Segrais's nerves, but he
has declared an implacable war on evil and practises all kinds
of mortifications and austerities, which force his normally
sharp-tongued superior to say one day: "My boy, our Lord is
not dissatisfied with you."

One night, on his way to an outlying hamlet, Donissan has
an encounter with the Devil, who appears in the form of a
horse-dealer: "a lively little man, now to the right, now to the
left of him, now in front, now behind." Bernanos succeeds in
conveying a forceful impression of evil, and in some ways
Donissan seems to have the worst of the encounter. Nevertheless, he is left with the gift of seeing into people's souls.
This same night he meets Mouchette, who now re-enters the
story, and tries to free her of the devil's presence. Later on,
she commits suicide; as she is dying, Donissan snatches her
away from her father and carries her to the nearby church,
in accordance with her wishes. This act is considered impru-
dent by Donissan's superiors, and he is sent off to a monastery.
Seven years later he is appointed parish priest of Lumbres. We
meet him again towards the end of his time at Lumbres where,
like the Curé d'Ars, he spends a great deal of time in the confessional and is regarded as a saint. He is called to the
bedside of a dying child, who is dead by the time he arrives.
He daringly tries to bring him back to life, but is frus-
trated by the Devil. He makes his way painfully back to
Lumbres, only to die in his confessional, where he is dis-

covered by Antoine Saint-Martin, a writer (modelled on Anatole France) who has been attracted to visit him by his reputation. The portrait of Saint-Martin is pitiless; Bernanos had no time at all for the sceptical intellectualism of men like France, Renan and Gide. *The Star of Satan* is not an easy book to read—the narrative is at times confused—but it succeeds brilliantly in evoking the supernatural realities behind everyday appearances and leaves an indelible impression on the reader's mind.

Bernanos' masterpiece is undoubtedly *Le Journal d'un Curé de Campagne* (Eng. tr. *The Diary of a Country Priest*), 1936. It was his own favourite. "I love this book," he once wrote, "as if it had been written by some one else. . . . If it is put before me on the day of judgement, I shall not dare to say to it 'I do not know you', for I know very well that it contains a part of my inmost being." The notion that a dying country priest would find the time, energy or inclination to note down his experiences and reactions right up to the moment of death in such detail takes a little swallowing, but most forms of literature are dependent on the acceptance of conventions, and this particular convention does enable Bernanos to take the reader straight to the heart of his subject—the struggle between holiness and humility on the one hand and pride and apathy on the other—and to keep him there. The climax of the poverty-striken Curé d'Ambricourt's efforts to make a success of his job as a parish priest in his interview with the local Comtesse. With words put into his mouth by God he is suddenly enabled to wean this aristocrat from the sterile devotion to the memory of a dead son, which for years has poisoned her relations with her daughter, and her whole attitude to life. After the Curé has left her, the Comtesse writes him a letter expressing her thanks:

Monsieur le Curé,

I don't suppose you can imagine my state of mind when you left me, since all such questions of psychology probably mean nothing at all to you. What can I say to you? I have lived in the most horrible solitude, alone with the desperate

memory of a child. And it seems to me that another child has
brought me to life again. I hope you won't be annoyed with
me for regarding you as a child. Because you are! May God
keep you one for ever! (Trans. Pamela Morris.)

The Curé slips this letter into his copy of the *Imitation*, but
his happiness is short-lived; the Comtesse dies of a heart
attack that same night and he is suspected of helping to bring
it on, for the interview has been overheard and misinterpreted.
However, he himself has not much longer to live; a visit to a
doctor in Lille discloses that he has cancer of the stomach; in
his pain and misery he takes refuge—unintentionally giving
scandal to the end—in the house of an unfrocked priest whom
he knew at the seminary, and dies there, without the last
sacraments, but muttering, "Does it matter? Grace is...
everywhere". The Curé d'Ambricourt embodies one side of
Bernanos' simple, direct and fervent Christianity; the other
side is represented by the bluff but sensitive Curé de Torcy,
who sees the worth of his young colleague and encourages
him to stick to his guns.

Bernanos wrote four novels in between *The Star of Satan*
and *The Diary of a Country Priest*. None of them is a complete success, and two of them must be regarded as failures.
Un Crime (Eng. tr., *A Crime*) (1935), and *Un Mauvais Rêve*,
which was written between 1931 and 1934, but only published
posthumously in 1951, may be summed up as attempts at
metaphysical thrillers—they have something in common with
Graham Greene's earlier books—but the characters are artificial and the books do not really "come off"; in fact, *Un
Mauvais Rêve* was never finished. The two earlier novels,
L'Imposture (1927) and *La Joie* (Eng. tr., *Joy*) (1929) both
introduce the extraordinary figure of Abbé Cénabre, a priest-
scholar whose cold scepticism has gradually killed all faith
and charity in him, leaving him an empty shell. Bernanos
himself once described *L'Imposture* as "a face of stone, but
one which weeps real tears". Cénabre, who in some ways is
reminiscent of Renan (but Renan left the seminary before
receiving major orders; Cénabre carries on as a priest though

he has no faith), reappears in *La Joie*, which forms a continuation of *L'Imposture*. He is saved when he hears of the
death of the saintly young Chantal de Clergerie, the heroine
of *La Joie*, who is murdered by the Russian chauffeur Fiodor,
a curiously artificial figure. He utters the first words of the
Lord's Prayer, then falls face forward and later dies in a
lunatic asylum without recovering his reason.

Bernanos was a socio-political pamphleteer as well as a
novelist; in this respect he has affinities with Belloc and
Chesterton, but even closer ones with Péguy. Like Péguy, he
dreamed and pleaded for the old Christian France. The first
book in which he put forward these views was *La Grande
Peur des Bien-Pensants* (1931); the most famous is *Les
Grands Cimetières sous La Lune* (Eng. tr., *A Diary of my
Times*) (1938). *La Grande Peur* starts off as a biography of
Edouard Drumont, the nineteenth-century anti-semite, whom
Bernanos saw as a typical representative of the old France
which was rapidly disappearing:

> He was a man from my part of the country, of the same
> stock as I am (or you are), a good strong Frenchman, with
> fairly broad shoulders and a firm step. Men like that look
> after their own affairs as long as they can stand upright. As
> long as they can stand upright they live their own lives, without
> asking anything of anyone; they carry good and evil, each in
> its place, so that God can see where he is more quickly on the
> day of judgement.

Les Grands Cimetières sous la Lune is a denunciation of the
excesses of the Nationalists in the Spanish Civil War. Bernanos,
who was living in Majorca at the time, began by supporting
Franco, and one of his sons enrolled in the Falange, but his
sympathies were soon alienated as he was unable to approve
of the behaviour of the Spanish Church. That Bernanos, a
right-wing monarchist, should have adopted this unorthodox
and courageous line, is typical of the man. Fundamentally he
belonged neither to the right nor to the left; he was interested
only in justice, and he wrote to rouse people in its interests.
"I have sworn to move you," he once said, "to friendship or

fury; it doesn't matter which." The title of *Les Grands Cimetières* refers to the vast resting-place of those who died in the First World War; like them, Bernanos had fought for a better world—more particularly, for a better France—but he had lived to be disappointed. One of his last polemical works was *La France contre les Robots* (1944), a denunciation of the enslavement of man by the machine; it is something of a rag-bag, but it contains some noble passages in Bernanos' most trenchant style:

> The Civilization of Machines is the civilization of quantity as opposed to that of quality. So the imbeciles [this is Bernanos' special word for all those he dislikes, like Sartre's *salauds*] dominate it by numbers; they *are* numbers. I have already said, I say again, and I shall go on repeating until the hangman knots the rope under my chin: a world dominated by force is an abominable world, but a world dominated by Numbers is ignoble.

If Bernanos has no very original solution for the complex problems of modern society, that is because he always remained a child, in the noblest sense of the word. He is at his best in describing the war between good and evil in the human heart. When one thinks of his novels, the first figures that rise before one are his priests. They are not the first priest-heroes in French literature—in the twentieth century alone, René Bazin, Paul Bourget, Camille Mayran, Robert Vallery-Radot and Léon Cathlin have all written novels round priests—but they are certainly the most vividly-drawn and distinctive ones, so much so that they have given rise to the phrase, "C'est un prêtre à la Bernanos." They are exceptional beings, priests, as it were, to the *n*th degree, reflecting Bernanos' own faith and hope.

In the last years of his life Bernanos turned to the drama and produced a work that is so near being a masterpiece that it seems likely that he could have been as successful in the theatre as he was with his best novels. The *Dialogues des Carmélites* (Eng. tr., *The Carmelites*) (1948) was written as the script for a film that in fact was never made. It is based partly on a historical fact, the martyrdom of the sixteen Carmelite nuns of Compiègne, who were guillotined on July 17th, 1794, and partly on the *Novelle* which the German writer Gertrud von le Fort wrote around it, *Die Letzte an Schafott* ("The Last at the Scaffold"). The central figure, a young aristocrat called Blanche de la Force, is Gertrud von le Fort's creation. The dominating element in Blanche's make-up is fear; borne prematurely soon after her mother had been frightened by a rioting crowd, she is so timorous that the servants call her "little hare". She joins the Carmelites to escape the rigours of life in society, but it is the period of the Revolution, the Terror breaks out and convents are dissolved. Blanche, still fear-ridden, has avoided making the vow of martyrdom that the other nuns embrace gladly. She goes into hiding, but when the other members of the community are arrested and condemned to the guillotine, she emerges from hiding to follow them at the last moment on to the scaffold. The "stage directions" for the last scene run as follows:

> One can only see the base of the scaffold, which the Sisters ascend one by one, still singing [the *Veni Creator*], but as they disappear the choir grows smaller. Finally there are only two voices, then one. But at this moment a fresh voice rises from another corner of the great square, a voice even clearer and more resolute than the others, yet with something child-like about it; and towards the scaffold, through the crowd which parts in silence to let her through, comes little Blanche de la Force. Her countenance is devoid of any trace of fear.

The *Dialogues des Carmélites* reads a little disjointedly—it is, after all, a film script—and to that extent is a less satisfying work of art than Gertrud von le Fort's *Novelle*, but the force and economy of the language are superb. Bernanos prefaced the text with a quotation from his own novel, *La Joie*, in praise of fear:

> In a sense, you see, Fear is nevertheless the daughter of God, redeemed on the evening of Good Friday. She is not fair to look upon—No!—now mocked, now cursed, rejected by every-

one.... Yet, make no mistake: she stands by the bedside at every death, she intercedes for man.

It seems that from about 1930 onwards Bernanos was dominated by fear, and did not hide the fact. One of his friends, Henry Jamet, says that he was afraid of sin, of the world, of war, and that he found it almost impossible to resist this fear; hence, no doubt, the attraction for him of the theme of the *Dialogues des Carmélites*, which may therefore be regarded as one of Bernanos' most personal and deeply-felt productions, and as an interesting example of the use of an objective theme to express subjective emotions.

MAXENCE VAN DER MEERSCH

Most of Bernanos' novels are set in the countryside of north-eastern France; those of Maxence van der Meersch (pen-name of Josef Cardijn, 1907–1951), are set in the big towns of the same region. Meersch was born near Roubaix, and had a profound understanding of the working classes of such towns. He started off as something of a Marxist, but eventually rejected this solution in favour of Christianity; *L'Elu* (*The Chosen One*) (1937) describes a conversion in a tone which suggests that it is autobiographical. This book stands apart from his other novels, which are written in the naturalistic style of Zola, though with a tinge of mysticism which has suggested comparisons with Dostoevsky and Tolstoy (though the comparison should not be taken to imply that Meersch is in the same class). A typical example is *Pêcheurs d'Hommes* (*Fishers of Men*) (1940), which describes the struggles of the J.O.C. (Young Christian Workers) against the socialists and communists in a big industrial town—Roubaix, in fact—with the great strike of 1936 as the climax. Meersch succeeds admirably in "getting under the skin" of the hero and narrator, a sickly but courageous young workman called Mardyck, whose naïve but intensely sincere and practical Christianity cannot but win the reader's sympathy. His name and that of his creator are

a reminder that in Meersch's novels we are among the people
of Flemish stock so often praised by Bernanos' robust Curé
de Torcy in *The Diary of a Country Priest*. The book closes
with Mardyck's lyrical reflections on the Young Christian
Worker movement:

> So far as I am concerned, it saved my youth. It snatched me
> from vice, from temptation, from degradation. It taught me to
> respect women, and the duties and joys of true love. I owe
> my happy marriage to it. I am indebted to it above all for a
> proper understanding of life and its purpose. . . . It has enabled
> me to really live my Christianity, and to grasp the full meaning
> of the command which sums up life: "Take up your cross and
> follow me."

It is perhaps unfair to quote this piece of edification out of
context; it is entirely "in character" in the book, and does not
disturb its artistic unity.

FRANÇOIS MAURIAC

Both Bernanos and Meersch—in his later novels, at any
rate—are "positively" Christian writers, the tenor of whose
books is quite clear and has never provoked criticism in
orthodox Catholic circles. This cannot be said of France's
greatest living Catholic novelist, François Mauriac, who has
been accused of "complicity" with the sins of his heroes and
heroines. Mauriac was born in 1885 of an upper middle class
Bordeaux family. It is with such families that his long series
of novels deals; most of them are set in Bordeaux or the
vineyards and pine-woods of the surrounding district, the
Landes. The first of these novels was *L'Enfant chargé de
chaînes* (Eng. tr., *The Child in Chains*) (1913); the most recent
is *L'Agneau* (Eng. tr., *The Lamb*) (1954). They won him a
place in the *Académie Française* in 1933, and the Nobel prize
for literature in 1952. Mauriac has also written a number of
plays, of which the best is probably *Asmodée* (1938); a good
deal of literary criticism (*La Vie de Jean Racine*, 1928; *Trois
grands hommes devant Dieu*, 1930); and a life of Jesus (1936).

For the last fifteen years or so his column in *Figaro*, and later in *L'Express*, has been one of the high-spots of French journalism.

The particular criticism of Mauriac that we mentioned above is summed up in the following extract from Pierre de Boisdeffrés *Métamorphose de la Littérature* (Paris, 1953): "Would it be exceeding the limits of criticism to point out to him [Mauriac] that Cybele and Christ have shared his work? Mauriac the novelist has little to do with Christianity (except perhaps in *Le Baiser du lépreux*)[3]; on the other hand, Mauriac the essayist and critic is a Catholic writer."

By and large, this charge is not true, but a novel like *Destins* (Eng. tr., *Lines of Life*) (1928)—from the point of view of artistry, one of Mauriac's most satisfying—makes it easy to see why it was made. It would be going too far to say that *Destins* is a *Hippolytus* or *Phèdre* in modern dress, but it certainly has affinities with the theme of these plays. Bob Lagave, the handsome, debauched grandson of an old family servant, comes to stay on Pierre Gornac's country estate to convalesce after a serious illness. Old Gornac's estate is managed by his capable daughter-in-law Elizabeth, whose husband is dead. She is forty-eight, and involuntarily attracted to the young Lagave, so that when he asks if he can entertain his girl-friend, Paule de la Sesque, daughter of a local family of some standing, she agrees to let her come for a day. Although, unlike Phèdre, Elizabeth Gornac connives at the two lovers' happiness, her feelings on that day are strongly reminiscent of those of Racine's heroine:

> She had always been struck by the supernatural stillness brooding over the vines on these torrid August afternoons, while, a few miles away, the living forests were dying in a vast crackling of burning wood. And today, she was more than

[3] Eng. tr. *A Kiss for the Leper*. In this brilliantly realistic novel, one of Mauriac's earliest, a young husband realizes that he repels his wife. He catches tuberculosis at the bedside of a dying friend, and dies himself. His wife remains faithful to his memory though she could easily have married again.

ever aware of the silence. Another fire, a very different fire, was smouldering close at hand, a few feet away, perhaps, behind the nearby privet. The forest blaze might, perhaps, spread towards Le Bos, but it was not of those thousands of trees that she was thinking now, but of two bodies, lying she knew not where—probably within a stone's throw—so near the path on which she was standing that, but for the south wind with its smell of burning resin, she might have heard . . . what might she have heard? (Trans. by Gerard Hopkins).

Although the emphasis is different, we cannot help being reminded of Phèdre's famous lines:

> Dans le fond des forêts allaient-ils se cacher?
> . . .
> Au moment que je parle, ah, mortelle pensée!
> . . .
> Ils font mille serments de ne se point quitter.
>
> (*Phèdre*, Act IV, Sc. 6)

That evening, Elizabeth's only surviving son, Pierre, who is presented at this stage as a prim prig, arrives home unexpectedly and is horrified to hear that Paule has been consorting with Bob Lagave. He loses no time in acquainting Paule with the unsavoury reputation which Bob Lagave enjoys in Paris, and she is so shocked that she decides to go off without seeing Bob (who is innocently asleep in his grandmother's cottage, happy in the thought that Paule loves him), and to think things over for a few weeks. Significantly, Elizabeth Gornac at this point takes Bob's side, rather than her son's, and says to Paule: "When one admits that one loves, there is no more to be said: in love there is room for everything, or so it seems to me. Respect for the man one loves? . . . Forgive me if I say that to me such words are quite meaningless."

Paule is unconvinced, and drives off early the next morning. Bob is at first puzzled by her sudden departure, but at the sight of Pierre Gornac, "that church-haunting beadle, that nauseating Tartuffe," he soon guesses what has happened. There is an ugly scene between the two young men, and Bob knocks Pierre down. He then takes refuge in drink, and when, after a fortnight, there is no news of Paule, he goes off with some of his Paris friends and is soon killed in a car accident, lingering on just long enough after the crash to make his peace with God. The person most affected by his death is Elizabeth Gornac; she goes to pray before Bob's coffin in the church the day before the funeral, and breaks down completely, to the horror of her son:

> Then, suddenly, he heard a long-drawn rattle in her throat, and saw that she was trembling all over. Her shoulders were twitching. She was breathless, and shaken by hiccups. She stayed like this until, at last, her body collapsed upon a chair, as under a rain of blows. The empty church echoed back her heavy sobbing. She made no attempt to wipe the tears from her cheeks, but one damp hand had disarranged her neat strands of hair. A single loose grey lock gave her an appearance of disarray and shame. In vain did Pierre tell her to lean upon his arm, and go with him. She seemed neither to hear nor to see. Thank God, there was nobody in the church but the dead man and the prostrate, shadowed figure keeping watch beside him [the dead man's grandmother]. It did not turn its head. But at any moment now, somebody might come in.
>
> "Come with me, mamma: let us not stay here."
>
> But, deaf to his voice, she half stretched her arm towards the coffin, stammering broken words, calling upon the mortal remains lying there before her (Trans. Gerard Hopkins).

In the months and years that follow, Elizabeth Gornac does not forget her love for Bob Lagave, but her other passion—for the land—reasserts itself, and she devotes herself again to running her father-in-law's estate. The novel ends with these sentences:

> At the hill of Viridis the coachman slowed down the horse to a walk. This was the spot on the road where she always remembered having once met Bob, when he was a child, on his way home from bathing, carrying his minute and dripping bathing shorts, and biting a black grape. She saw him again now. She also saw that the blight had destroyed her neighbour's vines, and rejoiced to think that Viridis had been spared. But she must see that Galbert gave them two more

sprayings. Elizabeth Gornac had again become one of those
dead who are carried down the stream of life (Trans. Gerard
Hopkins).

At first sight, Christianity does not emerge in a very convincing light from this skilful study of the last awakening of
love in an ageing woman's heart. In Bob Lagave, Christianity
is non-existent until the moment before death, in Pierre Gornac
it is blindly complacent and in his mother it is no match
for her physical passion. But this superficial view would be
grossly unfair to Mauriac. The masses of flowers sent by
anonymous friends for Bob Lagave's funeral are meant to
indicate that there was more good in him than most of his
relatives would allow; Pierre Gornac's smug Christianity
receives a double jolt from Bob Lagave's death and his
mother's behaviour that makes it far more profound; and
Elizabeth Gornac reveals a capacity for love that has taken
her closer to God, although she does not realize it: "God,
who, for her son Pierre, was Spirit and Life, in her was
numbness and sleep." In loving Bob Lagave, she had only
been following the law of her woman's nature; as the priest
to whom she confesses her love says, "You are all the same,
my poor daughter, when one knows one, one knows the lot".
Unpleasant though he is at his first appearance, it is Pierre,
his complacency shattered by the events of the story, who is
entrusted with the author's final comment on them: "One can
change nothing in human beings, nor can human beings change
themselves unless it be by the Creator's will operating in each
one of them. They must be ransomed as they are, with all
their load of propensities and vices; they must be taken,
ravished, saved, with all their sins still on them." (Trans.
Gerard Hopkins.) These words reflect the Jansenism that
tinges Mauriac's thought.

It seemed worth while to linger over *Destins*, because it is
one of the most difficult of Mauriac's novels to interpret. At
least the analysis has shown that Mauriac is far from mani-
pulating reality to prove any kind of a thesis; which in turn
illuminates his assertion that he is a Catholic who writes

novels rather than a Catholic novelist. Usually there is a fairly clear hint that the rebels against the stifling bourgeois society which he describes so convincingly are on the road to God. The heroine (or, in contemporary parlance, the anti-heroine) of *Thérèse Desqueyroux* (Eng. tr., *Thérèse*) (1927), who in a moment of desperation tries to poison her grossly insensitive husband, and Maria Cross, the kept woman of *Le Désert de l'Amour* (Eng. tr., *The Desert of Love*) (1924), are both nearer salvation than the society which rejects them. For to Mauriac, sin is not so much the positive temptation to evil which it is to Bernanos, as the absense of love; his attitude is mystical rather than moral. To that extent, dissatisfaction, in whatever form it is expressed, must be the first step on the road to God; the people who are really lost are those who are sunk in self-satisfaction, even, or perhaps especially, when it takes the form of a punctilious observance of the outward forms of religion. In a sense, most of Mauriac's novels could be described as studies in frustration or, better, divine discontent; they show us, not people being saved, but people in a frame of mind which makes salvation possible. One of the most positive conclusions is that of *Noeud de Vipères* (Eng. tr., *The Knot of Vipers*, 1932), the first novel that Mauriac wrote after a conversion that may be termed "Pascalian", for he has never been anything but a believing and practising Catholic. The embittered miser of whose journal the book consists eventually comes to see what Christianity can mean, and when he dies he is on the point of returning to the Church.

There is little development in Mauriac's career as a novelist. Apart from the first one or two novels, in which he was naturally finding his feet, the earlier ones, such as *Génétrix* (Eng. tr., *Genetrix*) (1923), a study of maternal domination, are as accomplished as the later ones. In fact, the most recent, *L'Agneau* (Eng. tr. *The Lamb*) (1954), which attempts a more positive picture of Christianity, with a would-be priest sacrificing his vocation on behalf of others, shows a certain confusion and loss of grip. They are all fairly short books,

compressed psychological studies in the classical tradition of
La Princesse de Clèves. That first great French novel was
fundamentally a Cornelian drama of will in narrative form;
Mauriac's novels are Racinian dramas of people carried away
by their passions, with the passions interpreted as signs of
grace rather than of damnation, against a background of the
Bordelais conveyed by a host of vivid but concise details
which make the characters grow, as it were, out of their environment.

Mauriac has thought and written a good deal about the
situation of the Christian who writes. We have already quoted
some of his remarks in the introduction to this book. Two
more deserve to be added. In 1933 he wrote:

> As a novelist, I realize today all that I owe to my Catholi-
> cism. I used to congratulate myself on having made some
> sacrifices to God in this field. But no! not even that ... Even
> on this level I owe all to Jesus Christ. It was the joy and the
> peace of his presence, and, alas! the anguish of his absence;
> it was the state of sin and the state of grace which made the
> day and the night of the humble world that I imagined—that
> darkness shot through with beams of light.

> [And more recently:] In sin or in the state of grace, funda-
> mentally I have never spoken of anything but Christ. Many
> have assured me, and still assure me, that he has made use
> of what I have written. If I have offended him, I have never
> denied him. From my childhood until now, I have never
> blushed at his name before others.

Coming from a man as courageous and honest as Mauriac,
these words must be taken into account in any assessment of
his novels.

JULIEN GREEN

The most striking fact about Julien Green (b. 1900), the
third of the three major Christian novelists which French
literature has thrown up in the last fifty years, is that by
birth he is an American. His parents, who were Southerners
from Virginia, settled in Paris in 1895; their house was furnished in a style typical of the old South, but Green was

educated at a French lycée and, except for a number of
sojourns in the United States—the longest was his war-time
exile from 1940–45—has lived all his life in France. All his
books except *Memoirs of Happy Days* (New York, 1942) have
been written in French, a French which, although perfectly
idiomatic, seems to reflect Green's foreign birth in its careful
precision and extreme lucidity.

Green's father was a Presbyterian, his mother an Episcopalian. His father eventually became a Catholic, and Green
followed him, quite independently, at the age of sixteen, under
the influence of Pascal and Cardinal Gibbons' *Faith of our
Fathers*. Nevertheless, some of his novels reflect the Calvinism
whose doctrine of predestination had driven some of the
nineteenth-century Greens into bouts of religious mania bor-
dering on madness. A good example of this, and of Green's
novels in general, is *Moïra* (Eng. tr., *Moira*) (1950), whose
setting—a university in one of the Southern states of the
U.S.A.—is no doubt based on Green's memories of his own
three years at the University of Virginia from 1919–1921.

The plot of the novel can be quickly told, for it is not only
a drama of crisis; the speed with which events develop is
positively hectic. A young man, Joseph Day, arrives at the
university from a quiet, conservative township in the hills. A
shock of red hair makes him a conspicuous figure, but he
has no desire to make many acquaintances, for the preoccupation of most of the students with sex horrifies him. By
choice as well as upbringing he is a puritan, who longs only
for the certainty that he is saved; at the same time, by temperament he is extremely passionate and comes near to murdering an aristocratic young Southerner called Praileau who
pulls his leg about his red hair.

Some students with whom he has clashed decide to play
a joke on him by sending a girl of easy morals to his room.
Moira arrives and locks herself in with him. For a long time
Joseph supports the situation admirably, but finally his passions are aroused and he yields to temptation; when he
awakes, he kills Moira. We have been prepared for this

dénouement by the fight with Praileau, but it still strikes the reader like a blow in the face. The view we are to take of Joseph Day is underlined by his friend's remark as he goes off to give himself up: "I don't judge you, I have never judged you. I've always thought that you were better than I am, I still think so. I shall never be anything but a little clergyman. But you . . ." The novel is a truly tragic treatment of awakening sexuality and the relation between God—a Barthian, "quite other" God—and the world.

Julien Green's novels have a unique flavour. Anchored in a precisely-observed reality—the house in the autobiographical *Le Voyageur sur la Terre* (Eng. tr. *The Traveller on Earth*) (1927) is the house of an aunt in Savannah, and the backcloth of *Mont Cinère* (Eng. tr. *Avarice House*), his first novel, is the estate of some American relatives whom he visited in 1919—a reality which is yet lent a timeless, universal air by the avoidance of proper names, they transcend this everyday reality to deal fundamentally with the mysterious, supernatural forces to which the characters are a prey. The writers of whom one thinks in connection with Green are Hawthorne, Poe and Blake. Many others, too, have contributed to form his thought and style, for he reads widely, especially the Bible (he learnt Hebrew to understand it better): "One must read the Bible continually," he says in his *Journal*, "to prevent the image of truth being obscured in us."

The typical Green character is a lonely individual who does not succeed in communicating with others, and indeed Green himself has asserted in *Memories of Happy Days* that solitude, the inability to communicate, is the theme not only of *Adrienne Mesurat* (Eng. tr. *The Closed Garden*) (1927) but of all his novels. The idea is summed-up in the title of one of his most recent, *Chaque Homme dans sa Nuit* (Eng. tr., *Each in his Darkness*) (1960), which seems to be the novel he was thinking of when he wrote in his *Journal* some years ago: "I should like to write the story of a man whose external appearance suggested a perfectly quiet mind, while in reality

this person's solitude was rendered tragic by carnal hunger."
Wilfred Ingram, with his "worried grey eyes", seems to his
relations to be a youth of blameless piety, though in reality
he is racked by physical desire. He inspires almost all those
who meet him to unburden their hearts to him: his dying
uncle Horace, his homosexual cousin, Angus, a young colleague at the store where he works and finally the mysterious
stranger, Max, who is possibly an incarnation of the Devil
but asks for—and obtains—forgiveness after shooting Wilfred
and inflicting a mortal wound on him.

During most of the book Wilfred is wondering how he
can seduce the wife of a distant relative whom he has met
at Uncle Horace's funeral, a Protestant who is attracted
against his will by the happiness of Wilfred's exemplary
Catholic death. Wilfred's character is summed up by his
cousin, Angus: "You are consumed by passions, but have
kept your faith in spite of it. That's what inspires me most
and what I envy you. Faith is stronger than everything else in
you" (Trans. Anne Green). *Each in his Darkness* is one of
Green's most highly elaborated and comprehensive books, yet
it retains the luminous—almost hallucinatory—simplicity that
characterizes all of them.

In recent years Green has also written three plays (*Sud*,
1953; *L'Ennemi*, 1954 and *L'Ombre*, 1956), but it may be
that the most enduring of all his work will be the *Journal*
which he has kept, with some breaks, since 1928. Six volumes
of it have so far been published. Like the novels, it is completely individual—there is no attempt to record daily happen-
ings or to register attitudes—and, like the novels again, it is
concerned above all to reach the reality behind the world
of appearances; it is a sort of spiritual autobiography, written
at first without any idea of publication. As the reticent style of
the novels shows, Green is the reverse of an exhibitionist.
Nevertheless, the *Journal* is completely frank, and allows us
to see the continual struggle in its author between carnal and
metaphysical reality. At the same time, it has a universal
quality, so that every reader can, as it were, participate in the

thoughts and emotions described. The following extract will give some idea of its quality and at the same time, with its summary of Green's feeling about religion, form a fitting conclusion to this sketch of his work:

> If I have ever taken anything seriously, it is religion. It is much more important to me than you would think. For me, it is linked to love, since it is mainly love. All the rest, brilliant and attractive though it may be, has never seemed anything more than an empty void, even when I yielded to the attraction of this void. (Journal IV, p. 174)

JOSEPH MALÈGUE

Bernanos, Mauriac, Green and van der Meersch were not the only Catholics writing novels in France between the two wars. A book that has been almost—and unjustly—forgotten is *Augustin ou le Maître est là* ("Augustine or the Master is There") (1933), by Joseph Malègue (1876–1940), who has been described as a Catholic Proust. *Augustin* is a long book of nearly nine hundred pages; obviously autobiographical, it describe's an intellectual's loss of faith through contact with modern exegesis, and his eventual return to the Church as a result of suffering; after seeing his mother and baby nephew die within a few days of each other, he himself collapses with tuberculosis and feels bound to renounce any thought of marrying the woman he loves. However, his conversion is not a retreat from thought to sentiment; suffering simply gives him the grace to see that the will is always involved as well as the mind, or, as Pascal puts it, "C'est le coeur qui sent Dieu et non la raison". Dying, Augustin dictates a new conclusion to his *Paralogismes de la Critique biblique*: "All the obscurities of Scripture and all its flashes of light will fall together, dragging each other, on one slope or the other, according to which side your heart is." *Augustin* is a leisurely book—it seems more like a product of the nineteenth than the twentieth century—but it is one that repays the reading; Malègue can paint a scene and create character as well as handle ideas.

Augustin also has historical interest and value in that it recreates the atmosphere of the Modernist crisis.

DANIEL-ROPS

Daniel-Rops (b. 1901), too, best known for his books on the history of Christianity, particularly *Jésus en son temps* (Eng. tr. *Jesus in His Time*) (1946), wrote a number of extremely competent if unexciting novels in the twenties and thirties. *Mort, où est ta victoire* (1934) is the story of Laure Malaussène, seduced physically and morally by Jean Paleyzieux, and saved by the prayers of Thierry in his monastery and the young Xave on her deathbed. *L'Epée de feu* (1939) describes the progress of a young man through communism, surrealism, and materialism to the Catholicism of Léon Bloy.

JEAN CAYROL

Since the Second World War, no young Christian novelist in France has achieved the fame of a Camus or the notoriety of a Sagan. Nevertheless, there are in fact successors to Bernanos, Mauriac and Green, namely, Jean Cayrol and Luc Estang, both of them influenced to some extent by the ideas of Emmanuel Mounier (1905–1950), the founder of the review *Esprit*, and of the philosophy called "Christian personalism". What these two novelists share with their three Catholic predecessors in the previous generation—and also with non-Christian writers like Sartre, Camus, Malraux and Anouilh— is the conviction that the quality which matters most is wholeheartedness, even when it is misdirected. This wholeheartedness can obviously take many different forms, but fundamentally what attracts Bernanos and Mauriac to sinners like Mouchette and Thérèse is the same thing that Anouilh proposes for our admiration in Antigone. The only people who are damned are the lukewarm and the compromisers.

Cayrol (b. 1911), who has published poetry as well as novels, is probably the more original writer, Estang (b. 1911) the more solidly competent novelist. Cayrol comes, like Mauriac, from Bordeaux, where before the war he was a librarian. He served in the Resistance, was arrested by the Gestapo and spent two years in Munthausen concentration camp. This experience must have provided the starting point for his surrealistic trilogy of novels, *Je vivrai l'amour des autres* (1947-50), which depicts the gradual re-acquisition of identity by a *clochard* or vagabond, a nameless deportee who wanders about the city like Lazarus risen from the grave. The first volume is a long monologue called *On vous parle*. By the end of the third volume the speaker has acquired a name, Armand, and there is an encounter with a priest; Armand retreats from this; but it is implied that he will not escape from God for ever. Like Camus, Cayrol has expressed his ideas in essays as well as in the form of novels; the concept underlying *Je vivrai l'amour des autres*, that of "Lazarus in our midst"— man disorientated in the modern world—is given philosopical form in the two essays collected in *Lazare parmi nous* (1950).

LUC ESTANG

The most substantial work that Luc Estang (b. 1911) has so far produced is the trilogy *Charges d'Âmes* (1949-54). It comprises *Les Stigmates* (Eng. tr., *The Stigmata*) (1949), *Cherchant qui dévorer* (Eng. tr., *Seeking whom he may Devour*) (1957) and *Les Fontaines du grand abîme* (Eng. tr., *The Fountains of the Great Abyss*) (1954), and deals with contemporary man's breakaway from, and hidden longing for, God. *Le Bonheur et le Salut* (Eng. tr., *Happiness and Salvation*) (1961) is an extremely honest and sensitive study of a scrupulous and inhibited Catholic's sudden abandonment of wife and family in an attempt to find happiness with another woman. The flash-backs to Octave Coltenceau's childhood form something of a link with the main theme of *Charges d'Âmes*, namely, the education of adolescents in Catholic schools. The last sentence of the epilogue strikes a rather unpleasantly complacent note. Octave's mistress has cut her own throat to avoid troubling his conscience further; he kneels by her bed, and "with his gaze fixed on the countenance of tortured love, he waits—with a new serenity."

GABRIEL MARCEL

But although both Cayrol and Estang have made their mark, the dominating figure in French Catholic literature and thought since the war has been a much older man, the philosopher Gabriel Marcel (b. 1889). Marcel, who became a convert to Catholicism in 1929, under the influence of Charles du Bos and François Mauriac, may be conveniently described as a Christian Existentialist; the main influences on his thought have been Karl Jaspers, Kierkegaard, Heidegger and Max Picard. For Marcel, existence is a cleavage between subject and object which demands that man should recognize —with faith—that there is an original totality. Such a philosophy, like Sartre's atheistic existentialism, clearly calls for concrete expression in imaginative literature as well as formal exposition, and in fact Marcel has written a whole series of plays, which, since the war, have all been staged with success. The earliest in date is *Un Homme de Dieu* (1925); one of the most recent, *Rome n'est plus dans Rome* (1951). In 1956 and 1957 Marcel gave two lectures on the connection between the theatre and religion (the first in Brussels, the second in Coburg); some of the remarks in them form an interesting commentary on the relationship between Christianity and literature which was suggested in the introduction to this book. Marcel puts his fundamental point like this:

> If the Christian drama is possible, that is because the very essence of the Christian religion is a drama; this drama is the Passion of Christ, the Passion of God Incarnate. Between Incarnation and Drama there exists an intimate connection which would be inconceivable in a religion of pure spirit, supposing that such a thing could exist and not be reduced to a philosophy; this connection is just as inconceivable in mythologies in which the god can take a human form but without

thereby becoming a man, disguising himself but not becoming incarnate.

If literature, for the Christian, must ultimately take a subordinate place to religion, it is just as certain that no religion or philosophy calls so insistently for embodiment and illumination in literary form.

Marcel's Christian existentialism is echoed in the novels of P. A. Lesort (b. 1915): *Les reins et les coeurs* (1946); *Le fil de la vie* (1951); and *Le vent souffle où il veut* (1954).

CHAPTER IV

GERMANY

After the end of the First World War there was a considerable upsurge of Christian literature in Germany. The theorists of this movement were Theodor Haecker and Romano Guardini, and a man who did a good deal to help it was a Viennese printer Jakob Hegner, who was to publish in Germany the books of Bernanos, Gilson, Reinhold Schneider, Edzard Schaper and many other Christian writers. The spirit behind the movement is summed up in this quotation from *Der weisse Reiter* (The White Horseman), a sort of symposium of young Catholic Expressionism published in 1920 under the editorship of Karl Gabriel Pfeill (1889–1942): "Decline or Christian renewal: that, it seems, is the enormous decision with which Christian civilization is now confronted." It would be pointless in a book of this size to list the contributors to *Der weisse Reiter*, for although their names are remembered in Germany their work made no impact outside its frontiers. In general, the same is true of the "peasant" or historical novels of "folk" writers like Max Mell, Regina Ullmann, Jakob Kneip and Paula Grogger. A fairly typical example of this kind of book is Paula Grogger's (b. 1892) *Das Grimmingtor* ("The Gate of Fury") (1926), a 600-page tale of the adventures of four brothers in the wars against Napoleon: the farmers are chips off the old block, the French wicked, the children innocent and the women pious. The fact is that for first-rate literature that is religious in inspiration we must turn in the first part of the century to the work of a Jew, Franz Kafka (1883–1924). It is unlikely that any certain interpretation of *Der Prozess* (Eng. tr., *The Trial*) (published posthumously in 1925) or *Das Schloss* (Eng. tr., *The Castle*) (1926), will ever be achieved, but the view that they deal with man's relation with God seen as Judgement and Grace seems to fit them extremely well.

If we change our standpoint and ask what major German writers in the last fifty years were, became or are Christians or near-Christians, the answer is "a great many". The list would include Gertrud von le Fort, Werner Bergengruen, Elisabeth Langgässer, Edzard Schaper, Reinhold Schneider, Rudolf Schröder, Heinrich Böll, Alfred Döblin and Franz Werfel (1890–1945), a Jew from Prague who wrote *Das Lied von Bernadette* (Eng. tr., *The Song of Bernadette*) (1942) in thanksgiving for his escape from France and the advancing Germans in 1940. But the Christianity of many of these writers does not show very clearly in their work (sometimes because, like Alfred Döblin, they joined the Church late in life when most of their work was already done); and even when it does, it has often been transposed into a bygone age. Attempts to interpret contemporary life in Christian terms are few and far between; Elisabeth Langgässer's novels are the most striking example. The popularity in modern German literature of the historical novel and *Novelle*, the long-short story centring round, in Goethe's phrase, "an unheard-of event that has actually happened", is striking; it is probably to be explained by the German fondness for symbols and schematic thought, by the attractions of the *Novelle* itself, which has been so popular in Germany since the Romantic age, and finally by the attitude of the Nazi régime to opposition, which made it necessary to disguise protests in historical dress.

GERTRUD VON LE FORT

Of the writers whose work is in fact positively Christian in tone, the most important is certainly Gertrud von le Fort (b. 1876), Germany's greatest living woman writer. Gertrud von le Fort was born in Minden in Westphalia. Her father was a Prussian officer whose family came originally from Savoy; her mother was a Protestant from Brandenburg. She studied theology under the Protestant theologian Ernst Troeltsch, who came to regard the inward piety of the mystics as the unifying element in Christianity and introduced her to Meister Eckhart, Jakob Böhme and Nikolaus of Cues. This approach led her towards Catholicism, and she joined the Church in 1927. It was her conversion that made her into a writer; what she wrote before this event attracted little attention and has since been suppressed by the author herself. Her remarks about the phenomenon of conversion are particularly interesting now that ecumenicism is being taken seriously by the Catholic Church as well as by the other Churches.

> The convert is not, as mistaken interpreters sometimes think, a person who emphasizes the painful denominational split, but on the contrary some one who has overcome it: his most real experience is not that of another faith to which he goes over, but that of the unity of the faith which submerges him. It is the experience of a child who realizes that his own most personal religious possession—the central Christian faith of Protestantism—as well as coming from the bosom of the Mother Church, is also preserved and protected in the bosom of the Mother Church. There is . . . a sudden recognition that the cleavage in faith is less a cleavage of belief than a cleavage of love, and that the theological conquest of the former can never succeed if it has not been preceded by the conquest of the latter.

Gertrud von le Fort has written poetry—for example *Hymnen an die Kirche* ("Hymns to the Church", 1924), a series of dialogues between the soul seeking God and the Church—but the bulk of her work takes the form of novels and *Novellen*. As we have already implied, most of these have a historical setting. A notable exception is her first novel— and main large-scale work—*Das Schweisstuch der Veronika* (Eng. tr., *The Sudarium of Veronica*), the first volume of which appeared in 1928, the second not until 1946. The heroine of this somewhat slow-moving *Bildungsroman* is an

orphan called Veronica who is brought up in pre-1914 Rome
by her grandmother and aunt. Her grandmother is more or
less of a pagan; her aunt and the housekeeper, Jeannette, are
Catholics. These two different philosophies are mirrored in
the buildings that surround the grandmother's house: on one
side the Pantheon, on the other the church of Santa Maria
sopra Minerva. As Veronica puts it, "I thus grew up between
two worlds, so to speak, which reached out for my young soul
not only invisibly and spiritually, but also in the shape of
living forms and mighty objects." Veronica's father has
ordered that she is to be brought up without any religion,
but her own experiences eventually lead her to become a
Catholic.

The setting of the second volume is Heidelberg just after
the First World War, where Veronica is attending lectures at
the university with her childhood sweetheart, Enzio, who has
returned from the war embittered at Germany's defeat. Enzio
may be regarded in fact as symbolizing the godless National
Socialist Germany which was to come into existence during
the next ten years. Veronica and Enzio become engaged, and
she tries to win him over to her own Christian, sacramental
view of marriage, but without success. Nevertheless, she sticks
to him, not only because she is deeply in love with him but
also because she feels that by marrying him she can share
God's grace with him. She is encouraged in this view by a
letter from her friend Jeannette in Rome, in which her former
spiritual adviser, the saintly Father Angelo, is quoted as
saying: "she (Veronica) has taken the only path that remains
to us: those who believe must enter the full communion of
love with those who do not believe." But her confessor in
Heidelberg regards this mystical approach as a dangerous one,
and when Enzio refuses even to accept the Church's conditions
for a mixed marriage, he warns Veronica that she is running
the risk of excommunication. His amazement at the boldness
of Veronica's theology of love is conveyed by means of a
pleasing and homely detail: "The gentle creaking of the
woodwork behind the grille (of the confessional) betrayed the

violence of his excitement." However, Veronica's faith is justified: the strain of divided loyalties brings on a nervous breakdown, and when she recovers Enzio begs her forgiveness for driving her so far. There is a rather implausible reconciliation and on this note of reunion and perfect love the book ends.

This second volume of the novel is in effect a long theological discussion conducted against the romantic background of old Heidelberg and the surrounding countryside, with Veronica's guardian, a liberal humanist professor of the old school, in the rôle of referee between his ward's Catholicism and Enzio's neo-Romantic nationalism. As a novel, it falls below the level of the first or "Roman" volume. Both volumes of *Das Schweisstuch der Veronika* are heavily loaded with symbolism, but the writing is lucid and natural, and the positive aspects of Christian love embodied in the attractive central character form a welcome complement to the portraits of frustration so frequent in Greene and Mauriac. Optimistic idealism is characteristic of German Christian writing, at any rate in the nineteenth century; it is the dominating note in the Austrian Stifter and the Swiss Gotthelf, though neither was blind to the darker side of life.

Both Gertrud von le Fort's other two novels, *Der Papst aus dem Ghetto* ("The Pope from the Ghetto", 1930) and *Die magdeburgische Hochzeit* ("The Magdeburg Wedding", 1938), are historical; so, too, are most of her *Novellen*. The two novels deal with Anacletus II, the Jewish pope who was set up as an anti-pope to Innocent II in 1130, and the capture of Protestant Magdeburg by Tilly's forces in the Thirty Years War. The first and possibly the best of the *Novellen* is *Die Letzte am Schafott* ("The Last at the Scaffold", 1931), which we have already mentioned as providing the starting-point of Bernanos' *Dialogues des Carmélites*. However, there are two important differences in the way these two works treat the story of the nuns of Compiègne. The first is theological. In Bernanos' play, there is a suggestion that Blanche is finally enabled to overcome her fear by the vicarious suffering of one

of the older members of the community on her death-bed; she
voluntarily assumes Blanche's fear, as it were. Gertrud von le
Fort has protested against this "distortion"; for her, the change
in Blanche is accomplished by "the pure, almost incomprehensible grace of God". In addition, the *Novelle* form permits
a more comprehensive treatment of the story and its historical
context.

Die Letzte am Schafott takes the form of a letter supposedly
written in 1794 from a Christian to an old friend, a lady who
believes in the nobility of human nature and its ability to
stand up to adversity without any supernatural help.

> Dear pupil of Rousseau, [writes the narrator at the beginning
> of the story] as always, I admire the cheerful and noble attitude
> of mind which enables you to go on believing in the indestruct-
> ible nobility of our nature even in the most dismal collapses
> of the human race. Yet, my friend, chaos, too, is nature, so are
> the executioners of your heroines [women like Marie An-
> toinette and Charlotte Corday], and the beast in man—so also
> are fear and terror!

The theme of Blanche's "deadly fear" is thus set in a frame
of the inadequacy of human nature as a whole, and the story
ends with the exclamation: "No, humanity alone is not enough
—not even enough for self-sacrifice." The Reign of Terror is
obviously a classic instance of the collapse of civilized values;
Gertrud von le Fort could hardly have foreseen in 1931 that
it was to be repeated so hideously in her own country. But the
horrors of the Nazi régime did not shatter her faith in her
fellow-countrymen. In *Unser Weg durch die Nacht* ("Our
Way through the Night", 1949), she protests against thinking
of "the Germans" as one homogeneous mass, and points out
that every country is a collection of individuals, some good,
some bad. This eminently sensible and Christian view finds
artistic expression in the *Novelle, Die Unschuldigen* (Eng. tr.,
The Innocents), one of the two stories in *Gelöschte Kerzen*
("Extinguished Candles") (1953).

The narrator is a boy, Harry, whose father, an officer in
the German army, committed suicide rather than carry out

an unjust and inhuman order. His mother is now being wooed by her husband's brother, Eberhard, and it gradually emerges that Eberhard was in command of the German troops who burnt down the church of Oradour in France, with all the women and children of the village inside it. An ancestor, the Commandant of Asslau, had committed a similar crime in the Thirty Years War:

> When the tower (of the Church) started burning, the bell fell down, the Commandant took it with him and when he got home, he made a present of it to the convent-church of Niederasslau; the first time it was rung in Niederasslau and the Commandant came into the church to hear Mass, the sound of it turned him crazy—he suddenly started laughing, as he did when he was outside the burning church, and he couldn't stop until he had laughed himself to death. And that is what will happen to every man of the Asslau family, they say, if he hears the Friederizia bell (Trans. H. M. Waidson).

The boy determines to ring the bell and drive his uncle Eberhard mad; the bell falls from the tower and kills the boy, but Eberhard slinks away from Niederasslau, and Harry's mother realizes that her child has saved her from a marriage in which she could never have found any real happiness. Harry joins the Holy Innocents, and all the children killed in the recent war, in Heaven.

The Innocents is a skilful blending of topical, historical and symbolical elements. Gertrud von le Fort's purely historical *Novellen*, such as *Das Gericht des Meeres* ("The Judgement of the Sea") (1943) can be stodgy—characters fail to come to life, the symbolism is too obvious and the language involved and heavy—but the best of them, on the other hand, are extremely moving. *Die Frau des Pilatus* ("Pilate's Wife") (1955) is an imaginary reconstruction of the lives of Pilate and his wife from the day of the Crucifixion onwards. The story is recounted by a Greek freedwoman of Pilate's in a letter to his wife's sister in Gaul. Pilate's wife, Claudia Procula, can never forget the look of mercy and forgiveness on Christ's face as he stood before Pilate in Jerusalem. She becomes con-

vinced of Christ's divinity and attends Christian gatherings in
Rome, but her love for her husband prevents her accepting
Baptism. She asks the leader of the Christian community if
Pilate's name can be removed from the Christian creed, and
is told that this is impossible. "Farewell," she replies, "I
sought here not the justice of God, but the mercy of Christ—
something that is not of this world—the quite other—but
you are just as blind to it as my husband was; you as well
as he caused the death of the Lord, and you are responsible
for it again at this moment, for you are abandoning his divine
mercy!" Claudia finally dies a martyr's death in the Neronian
persecution, after trying in vain to save her husband from
incurring fresh guilt by taking part in this persecution. Pilate,
seated at Nero's side, sees her die, and returns home resolved
to kill himself. He calls for his sword, but drops it when the
Greek freedwoman points out that, like Christ, his wife died
through him, but also for him.

Gertrud von le Fort is an uncompromisingly Christian
writer. Her particular contribution to Christian literature is
a sensitive and convincing picture of the rôle of women in
the economy of salvation. She can create women who are
holy but not priggish; Pilate's demure, devoted but dignified
Claudia Procula is a good example. A collection of essays
which she published in 1934 was called *Die ewige Frau* ("The
Eternal Woman"). The phrase is faintly reminiscent of
Goethe's "das ewig weibliche zieht uns hinan" ("the eternally
feminine draws us upward"), and this is in fact the theme
of much of Gertrud von le Fort's fiction. Classical in style,
romantic in content, idealistic in tone, it is very much in the
main stream of German literature. It is perhaps a pity that it
does not attempt more often to relate Christianity to contemporary life. Historical subjects make it easier to attain a
certain universality, but, used too often, they are apt on the
one hand to grow tedious, and on the other to give the
impression that the less tractable aspects of reality are being
deliberately avoided.

INA SEIDEL

Ina Seidel (b. 1886) is sometimes regarded as a Protestant counterpart to the Catholic Gertrud von le Fort. However, although both her grandfather and her husband were Protestant pastors, it is only in her later novels that Christianity plays a significant part. The themes of both her poetry and her long historical novel about the Napoleonic wars, *Das Wunschkind* ("The Love Child") (1930), are conjugal love and love for "Mother" earth, for one's country, one's homeland. *Das Wunschkind* is the story of a woman whose husband falls in battle; she tries to protect her son—conceived the night before her husband departed—from the same fate, but without success: "The day will come—and it must come —when the tears of women will be strong enough to quench the fire of war for ever." Christianity, rather than a sort of nature-mysticism, is more prominent in *Lennacker* ("The Lennacker Family"), another huge family chronicle which appeared in 1938. A student of medicine who has just returned from the First World War has a series of dreams, between Christmas and the Epiphany, in which twelve of his pastor-ancestors appear to him. The twelve separate stories form a history of German Protestantism from Luther to Adolf Harnach. A sequel, *Das unverwesliche Erbe* ("The Incorruptible Inheritance") (1954) traces the history of the distaff side of Lennacker's family and introduces Catholicism: his grandmother, brought up as a Catholic, is disowned by her father for marrying a Protestant—a reminder of the strength of inter-denominational feeling in the middle of the nineteenth century. Ina Seidel is a very professional novelist with a highly-developed talent for establishing character and atmosphere, and German Protestantism forms an important strand in the tradition which she is concerned to describe and defend, but Christianity is not the heart and soul of her work as it is in the cases of Gertrud von le Fort and Elisabeth Langgässer (1899–1950).

ELISABETH LANGGÄSSER

Elisabeth Langgässer was partly Jewish—in 1936 she was forbidden to publish by the Nazi régime, and her daughter was imprisoned at Auschwitz—and the tension between Judaism and Christianity is an important element in her books. Her best-known novel, *Das unauslösliche Siegel* ("The Indelible Seal", 1946), deals with the life of a Jew who becomes a Roman Catholic. Belfontaine cynically accepts the "indelible seal" of baptism in order to marry into a Catholic family, but remains a freethinker at heart. At the outbreak of the First World War he is on holiday in France. He is interned there, and after the war we meet him again living near Paris and married to a Frenchwoman; he has abandoned both his first wife and his faith. He is apparently enjoying his life of sin (or to him, of rational enjoyment) when he hears a voice calling to him from a thunderstorm: "Lazarus, come out!" It is his first wife, who has been murdered in 1925 and has now been granted the opportunity to save him ("the eternally feminine" again). He disappears, and turns up again in 1943 as an old Jewish beggar wandering about, rich in God's grace, between Russian concentration camps and Russian partisans; a sort of archetype of awoken and converted man (this is probably deliberate; the author suggests in an essay that the hero of the Christian novel will tend towards the archetypal because all Christians must die in Christ).

These are the bare facts of a narrative almost submerged beneath an enormous mass of symbolism and numerous digressions, which include the narration of the story of Bernadette. This rambling, discursive approach, with its jerky chronology—long periods of time are often passed over in silence—is no accident; it is based on a deliberate artistic theory. In Elisabeth Langgässer's view, the Christian novel should reflect the conflict between good and evil in form as well as content, and in a world in which the existentialist philosophies of thinkers like Husserl and Uexküll, and the scientific theories of men like Einstein, have upset traditional notions of time and causality, the traditional novel is no longer adequate to express the theme of the Christian novel, namely, "sin, grace and redemption" in the individual human soul. Elisabeth Langgässer propounded her conception of the Christian novel in two essays written towards the end of her life: *Grenzen und Möglichkeiten christlicher Dichtung* ("The Limits and Possibilities of Christian Literature") and *Die christliche Wirklichkeit und ihre dichterische Darstellung* ("Christian reality and its Literary Depiction"). In the first of these two essays she quotes with approval this passage from an essay by Eugen Gottlob Winkler[1]:

> The terminology of modern Catholic literary criticism divides Catholic novels into two categories, those which . . . are directly apologetic, salvationist and moral in effect, and those which depict what is in the Catholic sense evil, sinful, those which un-cover the temptations and abysses of human nature, in order to temper and harden Catholic truth by "a journey through Hell". In the latter case there arises, at any rate in the novel, an apparent indecision which, by leaving the natural, indubitable decision to the reader, creates a certain tension in him. This second path affords the more numerous and stronger artistic possibilities, as the work of Mauriac shows. Yet even Mauriac's novels are Catholic only in content and intention; they are not Catholic in nature and form, as for example the poetry and dramas of Henri Ghéon are. *The new form has still to be found.* . . . Only the kind of novel which is specifically Catholic in origin and nature . . . will, in so far as it is un-impeachable in its artistic principle and thus of guaranteed intellectual value, properly fulfil its apostolate for the Catholic idea in the realm of art.

Winkler's description of Mauriac's work is extremely apt, but his suggestion that the modern Catholic novel must find its own particular form is another matter. Elisabeth Lang-

---

[1] A Swiss critic who committed suicide in 1936, at the age of twenty-four, for much the same reasons as Kirilov in Dostoevsky's *The Possessed*—to win freedom in a chaotic creation by destroying himself.

gässer endorsed the idea—the italics are hers—and tried to put it into effect in *Das unauslösliche Siegel*, which ranges over space and time rather in the manner of Claudel's *Soulier de Satin* (she was undoubtedly influenced by Claudel and other writers of the *renouveau catholique*). The struggle between God and the Devil for Belfontaine's soul extends from the Pyrenees to Russia, and from 1858 to 1945. The result is a book which is often impressive but, as a whole, not easy to read.

Elisabeth Langgässer's last novel, *Märkische Argonautenfahrt* ("Arganauts' Journey in the March of Brandenburg", 1950), employs the same surrealistic technique. Seven citizens of Berlin undertake a pilgrimage in 1945 to a monastery in the Brandenburg village of Anastasiendorf ("the village of resurrection"); their goal is the golden fleece of divine grace. Again, the power of evil is emphasized: "God is condemned to failure—and whoever loves him is condemned to failure too. Failure is really the sign that one has been chosen." The final episode deals with the corruption of a boy by a gang of black market operators; it has suggested a comparison with Graham Greene. Langgässer and Greene certainly share a preoccupation with sex and violence, but there is a world of difference between the former's turgid and discursive style— *Das unauslösliche Siegel* may best be regarded as a sort of prose-poem—and the relatively direct and realistic narrative technique of the latter. Elisabeth Langgässer also wrote a good deal of poetry; two themes that recur in it are the notion —to be found a hundred years earlier in Annette von Droste-Hülshoff—that nature shares fallen man's guilt, and the attempt to incorporate pagan mythology in an all-embracing mystical Christian cosmology.

WERNER BERGENGRUEN

The fiction of Werner Bergengruen (b. 1892) is more relaxed in tone and traditional in form; like Stifter, Bergengruen is concerned to reveal "the eternal order which is reflected in the seasons of the year and the ages of the world, the lives of individuals and the destinies of peoples". Bergengruen (the name is Swedish) is a Balt from Riga, and he stresses that nostalgia for the Baltic lands is at the heart of his work. Several of his books were banned by the Nazi régime. He became a Catholic in the late nineteen-thirties, and his religious faith—particularly the ideas that God reconciles conflicting forces and that evil must be accepted as a necessary part of his plans—is reflected in most of the historical novels and *Novellen* that constitute the bulk of his work. The most famous of the novels is *Der Grosstyrann und das Gericht* (Eng. tr. *A Matter of Conscience*, 1935), which transposes (typically) the moral problems raised by the Nazi régime to Italy at the time of the Renaissance; it was widely read in Germany at the time.

The tyrannical ruler of a city-state orders his chief of police to solve a murder and produce the criminal. In reality the ruler himself has killed the monk Agostino, and has only instituted the inquiry in order to be able to study the reactions of his subjects. As subjects, they know only the power of the state; they obey, even when it involves betraying the truth. The ruler is equally guilty, for, intoxicated by power, he has arrogated to himself the divine privilege of leading people into temptation, of testing them, judging them and condemning them. The novel deals, says Bergengruen himself, "with the temptations of the powerful and the ease with which the weak and threatened can be led astray ..., in such a way that our belief in human perfection is dealt a blow. Perhaps it will be replaced by a belief in man's imperfection, for only in this belief can our perfection reside." *A Matter of Conscience* is a well-constructed novel—the atmosphere of tension and mystery is skilfully maintained—and one can understand the interest which it provoked in Nazi Germany, but it reads today rather too much like a demonstration; it never really comes to life.

The dominating idea in Bergengruen's work is that if a man confronts and accepts his destiny, then he will feel at home and at peace in a world which is ordered by God. This is the theme of his most substantial historical novel, *Am Himmel wie auf Erden* ("On Earth as it is in Heaven") (1940), which is set in Berlin in the sixteenth century. The Elector of Brandenburg's court astrologer, Carion, predicts a flood of biblical proportions which will destroy Berlin. The Elector Joachim tries to keep the prediction secret in order to prevent panic, but himself flees to the Tempelhof castle, the highest spot in the surrounding district. Events force him to realize that this was a dishonest thing to do, and he returns to the city to share the fate of his subjects there:

> Let the flood draw him down into its whirling depths, cast him against cliffs, carry him off to unknown coasts! He must find the freedom to entrust himself to the confusion of events, more, put out his arms eagerly to embrace them. He must renounce all safeguards, for only he who is willing to lose his life will gain it and find in the judgement of destiny a grace perhaps no longer expected.

There is, of course, no flood, but the court astrologer, Carion, who is as important a figure in the book as his master, the Elector, has to live henceforth with another fear, that of disease, for a rebellious leper flings an infected glove in his face. Carion overcomes this fear as his master overcame his fear of the flood: "He made the resolve, whatever might happen, to make a place for the will of the Divinity within his own will, and finally to let the latter be entirely consumed by the former. . . ."

The same notion of the necessity of facing one's destiny it at the back of the charming *Novelle, Der spanische Rosenstock* ("The Spanish Rose-bush") (1940), in which the rose-bush plays the part of a link between separated lovers: Lysander tells Oktavia that as long as the bush flourishes she will know that he is alive and well. Bergengruen has written a very large number of these shorter tales, and it is arguable that even his full-length novels are expanded *Novellen*, in that most of them centre round an individual event, like the murder in *Der Grosstyrann und das Gericht* and the expected flood in *Am Himmel wie auf Erden*. These tales are always entertaining—Bergengruen is a born story-teller with an apparently inexhaustible fund of material—but many of them are little more. The obedient acceptance of the world and everything in it tends to degenerate into a readiness to see everything through rose-coloured spectacles.

Bergengruen's lyric poetry (*Die Rose von Jericho*, 1936; *Dies Irae*, 1946), is mainly religious in inspiration; it seeks to show that "external events are only explanatory, coarsened images of the things that happen in men's souls."

EDZARD SCHAPER

Edzard Schaper (b. 1908) also has strong links with the Baltic countries, although he was born in Posen of a family that came from Hanover. He settled in Estonia in 1930 and lived there until 1940, when he went across to Finland as United Press Correspondent. He became a Finnish citizen, but eventually had to flee to Sweden to avoid being handed over to the Russians, who had condemned him to death. Since 1947 he has lived in Switzerland. By birth a Lutheran, he became a convert to Catholicism in 1951.

Schaper's novels deal with frontiers; frontiers between peoples and frontiers between ideas. Many of them have a historical setting—*Der Henker* ("The Hangman") (1940) is concerned with the conflict between Germans, Russians and the native population in the Baltic provinces in 1905–6; *Der Gouverneur* ("The Governor") (1954) is the story of a Swedish governor of the Baltic provinces when Sweden's power was declining at the beginning of the eighteenth cen-tury—but the most characteristic ones deal with the struggle between Christianity and Communism in eastern Europe in the thirties. *Die sterbende Kirche* ("The Dying Church") (1935) centres round the figure of Father Seraphim, the last priest of the once-great Russian Orthodox Church in Port Juminda, a little seaport in Estonia. The decaying fabric of his church symbolizes the decay of the Russian Orthodox Church in

Estonia, cut off from the Mother Church in Russia and hard-pressed by the Catholic and Protestant Churches.

Seraphim is an old man, but the last years of his life are not peaceful. His youngest son is fatally injured trying to steal the church vessels to prevent them being seized by the authorities in payment for overdue taxes, and when an elder and long-lost son suddenly appears unexpectedly he brings more sorrow than joy to Father Seraphim, for he is in reality a Soviet agent. After he has departed again in his fast motor-boat, amid a hail of shots from the Estonian police, Seraphim and his deacon, Sabbas, are arrested on suspicion of spying for the Russians. They are eventually cleared, but during their absence from Port Juminda their church has decayed still further, and at the climax of the Orthodox Church's great Easter liturgy the roof collapses, killing Seraphim and ten members of the congregation. It is the end of the Orthodox Church in Port Juminda, but not of the faith it transmits, for the saintly Seraphim has won over to Christianity the grand-daughter of an old Danish sea-captain, a girl brought up in Soviet Russia to laugh at priests; and his assistant, Sabbas, lives on to go back to Russia as a missionary.

Sabbas' story is told in *Der letzter Advent* ("The Last Advent") (1951), which forms a sequel to *Die sterbende Kirche*. In Russia he meets Seraphim's Communist son, and converts him to Christianity; the two die in a Russian prison. Schaper summed up the theme of this second book when he said: "There is only one kind of theology which is still convincing, and that is the theology of martyrdom, or shall we say that of the final personal example."

Die sterbende Kirche and *Der letzte Advent* lack the tautness of mood and construction of the really first-class novel, but they are lively, credible and readable treatments of a phase in the recent history of Christianity which is little known in the West, and this lends them a particular interest. Schaper has a deep and sympathetic understanding of the Orthodox Church; his only criticism is that it attaches too much importance to outward forms. The deacon Sabbas has clear evidence that the church at Port Juminda is liable to collapse at any moment—a lump of wood falls and inflicts a nasty wound on his head some time before the final disaster—but he keeps the knowledge to himself because he is afraid that if it is deprived of the visible symbol of its church the little Orthodox community will be scattered. It is to atone for this lack of faith that he feels compelled to return to almost certain death in the Soviet Union.

HEINRICH BÖLL

The Rhinelander Heinrich Böll (b. 1917), who has made a considerable reputation since the war with his novels and short stories, is a Catholic, but there is little positive evidence of the fact in his fiction, which deals mainly with the war and its aftermath in Germany in a brutally realistic way. What is quite clear is that Böll has little time for the outward manifestations of bourgeois Christianity. The war and what preceded it in Germany have left a far deeper mark on him than on any of the writers we have considered so far. *Wo Warst du Adam?* (Eng. tr., *Adam, Where Art Thou?*) (1955) describes the retreat of the German Army from Rumania; on the title page stands a quotation from Theodor Haecker: "A world catastrophe can be of great service. It can also serve as an alibi before God. 'Adam, where art thou?' 'I was in the world war'." The book consists of a series of tenuously connected pictures of what happens to various members of the retreating army. The central figure is an architect called Feinhals who is blown up by a German shell just as he is approaching his parents' house in the Rhineland. Just before this final demonstration of the futility of war he is made to say: "Then he wanted to go into the church, although he found it difficult to tolerate the faces of most of the priests and their sermons, but he wanted to do it in order to console God, perhaps also to console God for the faces and sermons of the priests." As a whole, the novel is laboured; the separate episodes are sharp and vivid, but they do not coalesce into an organic whole.

Billiard um halb zehn (Eng. tr., *Billiards at Half-past Nine*)
(1959) is a scathing indictment of the materialism of post-war
Germany. Again the construction leaves a good deal to be
desired; continual flash-backs make it difficult to see where the
book is going.

The key to Böll's attitude is to be found in his *Brief an
einen jungen Katholiken* ("Letter to a Young Catholic")
(1958) and the essay *Kunst und Religion* ("Art and Religion")
(1959). The "Letter" is addressed to a young man who has
just made one of the official one-day retreats arranged for
recruits about to join the army; Böll makes it the occasion for
a scorching attack on the attitude which emphasizes sexual
morality to the exclusion of the other aspects of morality. He
recalls a similar retreat he himself made in 1938:

> On the invitation there was something about "spiritual equip-
> ment for service in the army" . . .
> After breakfast came the spiritual equipment. The priest in
> charge of the retreat spoke first for roughly half an hour
> about the Centurion of Capharnaum, on whose frail shoulders
> it has been the custom for the last century or so to base the
> theological justification of compulsory military service. The
> dead cannot protect themselves, and the poor centurion had to
> go bail for all the slogans dealt out at that time: a people
> without living space, Bolshevist threat, a just war. Always look
> out, my young friend, when the theologians start talking about
> a just war. It is such a comprehensive and reasonable phrase
> that it really ought to be prohibited. The grandsons of the men
> who fell in 1914 are now being trained to use atomic canon,
> and after forty-four years the historians have still not agreed
> which side was fighting the just war. . . .
> The lecture on the Centurion of Capharnaum was followed
> by practical instruction which consisted in giving us advice
> on how to avoid drunkenness when we were compelled to
> attend regimental dinners and social evenings; it was important
> to take precautions against drunkenness because these celebra-
> tions were always followed by communal visits to brothels;
> the dangers of which we were warned were "moral" ones,
> which meant sexual ones.

By this time, the summer of 1938, most of my school friends had long ago left the various Catholic youth movements for the Hitler Youth or the *Jungvolk*; I used to see them sometimes, marching through the city at the head of their detachment. They would smile at me deprecatingly if their detachment happened to be singing "When Jewish blood spurts from the knife. . . ." I did not return the smile. I do not know which danger was morally greater: to sing "When Jewish blood spurts from the knife" with a hundred ten-year-olds or to commit a sexual misdemeanour.

It is in essays like this, and in the collections of short stories such as *Wanderer, kommst du nach Spa* (Eng. tr., *Traveller, If You Come to Spa*) (1950), that Böll's remorseless honesty and his gift for coining or fastening on a telling phrase are seen to their best advantage. Later in the *Brief an einen jungen Katholiken* he lashes his fellow-Catholics in a passage worthy of Swift. Apparently when the re-arming of Germany was being discussed, the headquarters of the Catholic youth movement issued a memorandum in which a good deal of attention was devoted to the practical qualities necessary in a prayer-book for soldiers; it was to be made more hard-wearing and solid by "good India paper and a flexible linen binding".

"These are precisely the things that German Catholics care about," says Böll,

> Every single phrase in this sentence—hard-wearing, solid, good India paper, flexible linen binding—is almost worth a pamphlet to itself. I have seen too many men die in Russia, both in battle and in hospitals, to be able to regard this sentence as anything but a devilish blasphemy, whose roots I am bound to seek in the dilettantism of German Catholics.

For Böll, the one important thing is to act in accordance with one's conscience; it was conscience, he points out, not the command of the official Catholic Church in Germany, that inspired Father Delp and all the many other Catholics who suffered and died in Hitler's prisons and concentration camps. Conscience, too, must determine the artist's attitude to his work. "The Churches may still be entitled to decide," says Böll in *Kunst und Religion*, "whether some one is a Christian (the Recording Angel can confirm or annul the verdict); but the Churches are not entitled to decide whether some one is an artist." In Böll's view, the terms "Christian author" and "Christian literature" are bandied about rather too freely. Anyone who gives himself out as a Christian and a writer ought to know where these two obligations will lead him; but he does not know, and no one can tell him. "So long as the secret of art remains undeciphered," Böll declares, "the Christian has only one instrument at his disposal, his conscience; but he has a conscience as a Christian and one as an artist, and these two consciences are not always in agreement." As a result, one can be a Christian and at the same time an artist, yet not a Christian artist. Any writer worth his salt must demand the sort of freedom so firmly defended in this essay, and we have already heard Julien Green, François Mauriac and Graham Greene using the same sort of language.

Yet in the last analysis there should be no cleavage between what a man believes and what he writes; if there is little positive trace of the former in the latter—and this is often the case with Böll's novel's—the result is bound to be work that seems to lack a dimension. Böll's satirical short stories are excellent; his novels are less satisfying. It is only fair to add that they are honest pictures of life in post-war Germany—Böll has described the writer as the man who *sees* the things and people around him—and that, by implication, they champion basic Christian ideals like family life. Böll has seen too much avoidable human misery—children without food, homes without husbands or fathers—to be concerned with subtle theological concepts.

REINHOLD SCHNEIDER

Reinhold Schneider (1903–58), whose father was the proprietor of the famous *Maison Messmer* hotel in Baden-Baden, was another of the many Germany writers of the last fifty years who have chosen to clothe their thought in historical forms. He was brought up as a Catholic, but tells us in his autobiography *Verhüllter Tag* (Overcast Day, 1956) that he was, as it were, reconverted later in life, largely under the influence of Unamuno. This path led, he says, "from tragic nihilism to belief, from independence to the acceptance of obligations, from subjective confusion to the historical". Elsewhere he describes the Christian writer as "simply a witness, not by intention, but by his mere existence. He is . . . the sower of disquiet, the accuser, the worm in the conscience." Schneider is primarily an interpreter of history; the theme of all his studies—for example, *Philipp der Zweite oder Religion und Macht* ("Philip the Second or Religion and Power", 1931); *Die Hohenzollern* ("The Hohenzollerns", 1933)—is the conflict between might and right, Christianity and the world. His oblique criticism of the Nazi régime did not pass unnoticed by the authorities; in 1941 he was forbidden to publish anything; in 1943 he was accused of "defeatism", and in 1945 of "making preparations to commit high treason". He managed to escape to Switzerland.

Schneider's most concentrated and effective exposition of his theme is the story *Las Casas vor Karl V* ("Las Casas before Charles V", 1938). Half fiction, half fact, it tells the gruesome tale of the Spanish colonists' cruel treatment of the American Indians; its climax is a description of the Council of Valladolid in 1550, at which the Dominican friar Las Casas pleaded that the Indians should be treated as human beings, not cattle. *Las Casas vor Karl V* is a slow-moving and doctrinaire piece of work, although Schneider injects a certain amount of life into it by introducing the figure of a repentant nobleman, Bernardino, who tells Las Casas the story of his piratical career as the two of them sail home from the Caribbean. Since Schneider wrote this story, the theme of Spain's colonial policy has been treated in a much livelier fashion by the Austrian dramatist Fritz Hochwälder (b. 1911), whose play about the Jesuit state in Paraguay, *Das heilige Experi-*

ment (Eng. tr., *The Strong are Lonely*) (1942), scored a deserved success in the fifties throughout Western Europe.

Except for Ina Seidel, the German writers discussed so far have all been Catholics. We come now to three Protestants who, if not of the same stature as Gertrud von le Fort or Werner Bergengruen, nevertheless enjoy substantial reputations in Germany.

RUDOLF ALEXANDER SCHRÖDER

Rudolf Alexander Schröder (b. 1878) is the oldest of the three. He can best be described as a Christian humanist who has made it his business to hand on the western tradition by translating Homer, Virgil, Horace, Shakespeare, Pope, Racine and Molière. As a poet, he has modelled his religious verse on the hymns of Gerhardt and Fleming, and he has been called "the poet laureate of the German Protestant community". Most of his prose is criticism, but he has told the story of his youth in *Der Wanderer und die Heimat* ("The Wanderer and the Homeland", 1931) and *Aus Kindheit und Jugend* ("Memories of Childhood and Youth", 1934). Schröder's work is often not much more than edifying popular and proverbial wisdom.

ALBRECHT GOES

Albrecht Goes (b. 1908) is the son of a Swabian pastor, and was a Lutheran minister himself until 1954, when he resigned his living to devote himself entirely to letters. During the Second World War he served as a chaplain with the German Army, and his experiences on the Russian front are reflected in the story *Unruhige Nacht* ("Restless Night") (1950), in which a Lutheran chaplain has to comfort the last hours of a young soldier due to be shot for desertion. The most striking of Goes' *Novellen* is *Das Brandopfer* ("The Burnt Offering", 1954), which deals with the persecution of the Jews in Nazi Germany. Jews had to collect their meat-ration from certain butchers at certain times, and the woman (an Aryan) who keeps one of these specially-designated shops is so horrified at the sufferings of the Jews who come to her shop that during an air-raid she decides to sacrifice her own life in expiation for the crimes of her countrymen. She is saved, but a scar on her face serves as a permanent reminder of her attempted act of atonement, and "as a sign of love, that love which upholds the world". This story of less than fifty pages is a vivid and realistic evocation of one of the most unpleasant aspects of Nazi Germany. The butcher's wife is clearly a symbol of the nobler side of the German people, a product of that urge to shed some of the guilt engendered by the Nazi period which re-appears again and again in post-war German literature.

This urge is at the bottom of Thomas Mann's novel *Doktor Faustus* (Eng. tr., *Dr. Faustus*) (1947), which presents Germany as a Faust in the power of the Devil; it led Werner Bergengruen to write a poem calling on the peoples of the earth to repent for the guilt they incurred by not preventing Germany acting as she did; and it has appeared again recently, in a still more surprising form, in Rolf Hochhuth's play *Der Stellvertreter* ("The Representative") (1963), which seeks to suggest that Pope Pius XII could have halted the wholesale massacres of Jews if he had openly condemned them.

MANFRED HAUSMANN

Manfred Hausmann (b. 1898) started out as a freethinker and was converted to Christianity by reading Kierkegaard and Karl Barth. This North German writer—he was born in Cassel and educated in Göttingen—made his name with a picaresque novel called *Lampioon küsst Mädchen und kleine Birken* ("Lampioon Kisses Girls and Little Birch Trees", 1928); Lampioon is the traditional German wanderer who roams the roads, enjoying the beauties of the countryside and kissing all the girls he meets. Hausmann's return to orthodox religion via Kierkegaard is marked by the story *Der Überfall* ("The Attack") (1944), in which a young artist has a vivid experience

of God and is forced to doubt whether he can be an artist—
a dealer in the illusory—as well as a servant of God. In recent
years Hausmann has produced a good deal of religious
drama: *Das Worpsweder Hirtenspiel* (1946) is a Nativity play
which has been frequently performed in German churches;
Aufruhr in der Marktkirche ("Uproar in the Market Church")
(1957) is set in Hanover in 1533 and portrays the conflicts
of the Reformation period. The cast of Hausmann's religious
thought is indicated by the fact that he wrote an appreciation
of Karl Barth to celebrate the Swiss theologian's seventieth
birthday.

STEFAN ANDRES

Many other German writers of the last fifty years have
touched on religious themes; one particularly interesting
example is the *Novelle, Wir sind Utopia* ("We are Utopia",
1943), by Stefan Andres (b. 1906). A renegade monk captured
by the enemy in the Spanish Civil War is saved by the grace
of God from murdering the lieutenant in charge of the
prisoners when he asks the monk to hear his confession, although by yielding to the temptation the monk could save
himself and his comrades from being shot. Andres, a Catholic
from the Rhineland, intended as a boy to become a priest
himself, and one of the devices he uses to maintain the tension is a discussion between the monk and the lieutenant on
the nature and implications of the sacrament of penance.

CHAPTER V

ITALY

Not surprisingly perhaps, those countries in which the Church remains most firmly established have least to show in recent years in the way of Christian literature. Hostile reaction to environment is the commonest of human characteristics, especially in intellectuals.

GIOVANNI PAPINI

Modern Italy is even poorer than Spain in first-class Christian writers; loss of faith in Catholicism seems to lead at once in Italy to a Leopardi-like pessimism. At the beginning of the century Antonio Fogazzaro (1842–1911), in his novel *Il Santo* (Eng. tr., *The Saint*, 1905), dealt with the question of bringing the Church up to date—the hero, a sort of lay evangelist, has a private interview with the pope and urges him to free the Church from falsehood, clerical domination, avarice and inertia—and, not surprisingly, was rewarded for his pains by seeing *Il Santo* placed on the Index. But Fogazzaro lived most of his life in the nineteenth century; the most considerable avowedly Christian writer of this century—and a not very attractive or impressive one—is the Florentine Giovanni Papini (1881–1956). Papini was an exhibitionist. He began his career as a futurist, anxious to abolish the dead weight of the past, and in his autobiography *Un Uomo Finito* ("A Man who has Failed", 1912), published when he was thirty-one, he described himself as a man "for whom God has never existed". However, soon after the Great War Papini, always a man of strong likes and dislikes—the most characteristic of his books are three collections of emotional, subjective critical essays, *Ventiquattro Cervelli* ("Twenty-Four Minds") (1912), *Stroncature* ("Slashings") (1916) and *Testimonianze* (Testimonies, 1918)—was converted to Christianity and signalized the event with his *Storia di Cristo* (Eng. tr., *The Story of Christ*, 1921), a realistic, vivid but often rhetorical re-telling of the Gospel story interspersed with sharp attacks on those who reject Christianity. The book ends with a prayer to Christ which includes a passionate and highly-coloured denunciation of the present (1921) state of the world:

> For four long years the world stained itself with blood to decide who should have the broadest lands, the greatest riches. The servants of Mammon sent Caliban to rot in interminable trenches that they themselves might acquire still greater wealth and impoverish their enemies. But this awful experience has been of no avail. Poorer and more famished than before, all nations have returned to prostrate themselves before the great clay-footed god whose name is Trade, upon whose altars they are ready to sacrifice their own peace and the lives of others. Business and holy Money dominate the minds of men more strongly than ever before. (Trans. Mary Prichard Agnetti.)

The element of truth in this tirade is almost obscured by the lushness of the language.

The most interesting of Papini's later books is *Il Diabolo* (Eng. tr., *The Devil: Notes for a Future Diabology*, 1955), in which he studies "the causes of Lucifer's revolt". Like Goethe in the Prologue to *Faust*, Papini believes that the relations between God and the Devil are "far more cordial than imagined", and suggests that Christians could help him, by their love, to save himself and once again to become, as he once was, the finest of the heavenly spirits: "If Satan can be freed from the hatred of Christians, men would be freed for ever from Satan." Papini ends his preface to this theologically unorthodox but stimulating investigation into the nature of evil with a quotation from Graham Greene:

> Where God is most present, there also is his enemy; and, on the other hand, where the enemy is absent, we will some-

times despair of finding God. One would be tempted to believe that Evil is only the shadow cast by the Good, in its perfection, and that we shall one day come to understand even the shadow.

CARLO COCCIOLI

Another writer in whose work the Devil makes frequent appearances is the novelist Carlo Coccioli (b. 1920), who has attracted more attention outside than inside Italy and since 1956 has written in French (e.g. *Manuel le Mexicain*, 1956, an interpretation of Mexico in terms of the tension between native myth and Christianity).

Il Cielo e la Terra (Heaven and Earth, 1956) is the story of an imperfect yet saintly priest—"a bridge between heaven and earth"—who at one point attributes his very vocation to Satan. It is certainly after witnessing a successful exorcism that he decides to enter a seminary. As a curate, Don Ardito Piccardi—the "novel" is based on the life of a real priest—tells his first parish priest that "Satan has taken possession of this parish and every one of us,"[1] and proceeds to describe present-day Christian society as "a decayed corpse". He is appointed parish priest of the mountain village of Chiarotorre, where he converts an atheist, heals a paralysed boy after a young girl has had a vision of Our Lady, and involuntarily drives a homosexual to suicide. He is not loved by his flock because he makes too many demands both on them and himself; he does not know how to inspire love. He is moved to the city, where he becomes a successful lecturer and writes on spiritual matters, but still finds no peace of mind. He returns to Chiarotorre in 1943, and there he is shot by the Germans because he insists on taking the blame when five German soldiers are blown up by partisans.

Il Cielo e la Terra is bound to remind us of Bernanos' *Diary of a Country Priest* (and also of *Sous le soleil de Satan*), but there are important differences. The central figure is an intel-

----

[1] Trans. Frances Frenaye.

lectual, whose mental horizon is a good deal wider than that of the Curé of Ambricourt, and he is seen through the eyes of several other pople as well as his own. Coccioli gives us letters from Don Ardito to the director of the Diocesan seminary, but also the reports and reminiscences of other figures in the story, including extracts from the suicide's diary. The result is a book that lacks the burning simplicity of *A Diary of a Country Priest*, but is wider in scope and makes a brave attempt to illuminate problems like homosexuality, the significance of extreme poverty and the whole question of divided personality: Don Ardito comes to the conclusion that Satan is one of the two halves into which each man is divided.

In *La Piccola Valle di Dio* (1948) (Eng. tr., *The Little Valley of God*), the natural and the supernatural mix on the easiest of terms. In this picture of the loves and hates of an Italian valley, which, we are expressly told, stands for Italy as a whole, Christ visits the earth again in the guise of a farm labourer, raises a child from the dead, saves a girl from an angry mob and changes the heart of a prostitute significantly called Maddalena Amato. Once again we have an exorcism—described in vivid detail—and considerable emphasis on the activity of Satan: "I think," says one of the characters, "that a great Presence has summoned Satan into this neighbourhood. I believe that this presence is watching us. Satan is but the shadow of God, and God will vanquish him. They are fighting for possession of the Temple...."[2]

From time to time the author steps out of the story to comment in an ironical or whimsical way on the doings of his characters. These passages are often rather tiresome, and, in general, the bones of the mythical element which Thomas Mann considers so necessary to modern "epic" (that is, narrative) literature stick out rather obviously from the flesh of the story, but, all the same, *The Little Valley of God* is an original and by no means entirely unsuccessful attempt to see life *sub specie aeternitatis*.

[2] Trans. Campbell Nairne.

UGO BETTI

The Christianity of Ugo Betti (1891–1953), the most substantial dramatist of twentieth-century Italy after Pirandello (many Italians consider him a finer dramatist than Pirandello), is less flamboyant, but fundamental to his work. Betti was a judge, with ample opportunities to study human weakness, and the theme of his serious plays (he wrote few comedies) is man's need for purification and harmony with God. This theme is worked out in terms of human psychology without any ecclesiastical or supernatural apparatus. Betti wrote about twenty-five plays, thirteen of them between 1939 and his death in 1953. They are dramas of crisis, set against a generalized background; there are no indications of time or place. The most successful was *Corruzione al Palazzo di Giustizia* ("Corruption at the Palace of Justice", 1944), which deals with the nature of human justice; perhaps the finest is *La Regina e gli Insorti* (Eng. tr., *The Queen and the Rebels*, 1949). The scene is a hall in a public building near the frontier; there has been a revolution, and travellers have been held up because the party in power suspects that the erstwhile queen of the country is among them. She is indeed there, disguised as a peasant woman, but a prostitute called Argia is mistaken for her. When her lover refuses, from fear, to identify her, Argia accepts the part thrust on her, rises superior to her past life and to those about her, and dies like a true queen:

> I believe that the Lord (she says), in a short time from now, will not be asking names of me; He will be asking what my profit has been. The only one I have had I have had this night. . . .
> I believe that God . . . has intentionally made us, not docile, for that He would find useless . . . but different from Himself and a little too proud . . . so that we may . . . stand against Him, thwart Him, amaze Him. . . . Perhaps that is his purpose. It is a long struggle. Only at the end do we find reconciliation; and rest (Trans. Henry Reed).

CHAPTER VI

SPAIN

That Spain has produced little in the way of vigorous Christian literature in the last hundred years is perhaps ultimately due to the dominating position enjoyed by the Church in Spain from the sixteenth century onwards. The alliance of Church and State led to obscurantism, intolerance and persecution which kept Spain behind the rest of Europe and provoked the liveliest minds into espousing the political and religious liberalism which seemed to have worked so well on the other side of the Pyrenees. But this in turn led to a reaction in defence of essentially Spanish values—conceived as spiritual as opposed to material ones—so that eventually we find Unamuno demanding the "Hispanization" of Europe rather than the "Europeanization" of Spain.[1]

MIGUEL DE UNAMUNO

Miguel de Unamuno (1864–1936) is an extremely interesting figure, but not an easy one to sum up. This Basque, who spent most of his life teaching Greek at Salamanca University (from 1900 onwards he was Rector of the University), was certainly not an orthodox Christian, yet equally certainly not a materialist; he wrote plays, poetry and novels, yet was not primarily a literary figure; and he talked metaphysics all his life, yet was not a philosopher in the academic sense of the term. Perhaps he can most fairly be called a poetic philoso-

[1] See *"The Roots of the Spanish Dilemma,"* by Professor A. A. Parker, in *The Cambridge Journal*, Vol. VI, no. 8 (May, 1953).

pher; a man whose main gift consisted in the ability to clothe a small number of deeply-felt ideas in wonderfully varied, vigorous, poetic—and untranslatable—language.

The central notion in Unamuno's thought is man's hunger for immortality and hence his need for God in order to have some guarantee of immortality. This half-religious, half-philosophical idea is discussed and developed with a wealth of erudition in Unamuno's most characteristic work, the long prose essay or meditation entitled *Del Sentimiento Trágico de la Vida* (Eng. tr., *The Tragic Sense of Life*, 1913). "We do not need God", says Unamuno towards the end of this book,

in order that he may teach us the truth of things, or the beauty of them, or in order that he may safeguard morality by means of a system of penalties and punishments, but in order that He may save us, in order that He may not let us die utterly. And because this unique longing is the longing of each and every normal man—those who are abnormal by reason of their barbarism or their hyperculture may be left out of the reckoning—it is universal and normative.

Religion, therefore, is a transcendental economy, or, if you like, metaphysic.[2]

The novel *San Manuel Bueno Martir* (Eng. tr., *St Manuel Bueno, Martyr*, 1931), Unamuno's last and perhaps greatest piece of creative work, continues the struggle with the problem of immortality. More of a prose poem or idyll than a novel in the normal sense of the term, it is the story of a priest, Don Manuel Bueno, related in retrospect by one Angela Carballino, who regards Don Manuel as her spiritual father. The philosophical core of the book is the priest's notion that immortality does not necessarily imply the continuation of one's human personality; the physical setting is a village by a lake whose waters are said to cover a buried city. Don Manuel's martyrdom is his obedience to the idea that his "self" must be "selfless" both in time and in eternity. His life is a practical demonstration of charity in that he refuses to disturb

[2] Trans. J. E. Crawford Flitch (a translation revised by Unamuno himself).

the simple faith of his parishioners by worrying them with his own doubts about a personal resurrection. He himself gives up the idea of a material personality in favour of that of a spiritual personality which he can only dimly understand. He says to Angela's brother, Lazaro, "My life, Lazaro, is a sort of continuous suicide, a struggle against suicide, which is the same thing"; and as death draws near, he says to Angela "Pray for us ... and pray also for Our Lord Jesus Christ" (whom Unamuno saw as a sort of struggling hero who attained immortality for the human race by his sufferings). Looking back on Don Manuel's life, Angela sums it up in this way: "One must live! And he taught me to live, to feel life, to submerge oneself in the soul of the mountain, in the soul of the lake, in the soul of the villagers, to lose oneself in these souls in order to remain in them".

It is clear that, in spite of his attachment to the figure of Christ (*El Cristo de Velázquez* is one of the finest religious poems in the Spanish language), Unamuno was by no means an orthodox Christian, but rather a sceptic seeking a faith. What he really wanted from religion was simply the assurance that his own strong personality would not disintegrate at death.

GABRIEL MIRÓ

Gabriel Miró (1879–1930), who died six years before Unamuno, wrote some of the most mellifluous Spanish of the century. His *Figuras de la Pasión del Señor* (1916) ("Figures from the Passion of Our Lord") is the story of Christ's passion transposed to eastern Spain, with more emphasis on the human than the divine element. The two novels *Nuestro Padre San Daniel* (1921) (Eng. tr., *Our Father Saint Daniel*) and *El obispo leproso* (1926) ("The Leper Bishop") are set in a small cathedral city in eastern Spain—a sort of Catholic, Spanish Barchester—and deal with the social and ecclesiastical intrigues that thrive in such places and the limited conceptions of religion usually displayed by those who conduct them.

JOSÉ MARÍA GIRONELLA

Anyone who wishes to gain some idea of the atmosphere in Spain in the years before the Civil War could do worse than read *Los cipreses creen en Dios* (1953: Eng. tr., *The Cypresses Believe in God*, 1955) a novel by José María Gironella (b. 1917) of such scope and length (nearly a thousand pages) that it has provoked a comparison with *War and Peace*. The book tells the story of the Alvear family, who live in the Catalan town of Gerona, from April 1931 to July 1936. There are five in the Alvear family: the father, Matías, a born republican and anti-clerical won over to belief in God by his wife; his wife Carmen Elgazu, a devout Basque whose chief concern is that her children should never lose the faith in which she has carefully brought them up; and the three children—two boys and a girl—Ignacio, César and Pilar. The Alvears and their many friends and acquaintances represent between them about every shade of political and philosophical opinion, and all these attitudes are presented objectively and sympathetically. Many of the characters are seen through the eyes of the eldest son, Ignacio, whose development from childhood to maturity is one of the subsidiary themes of the novel. Its climax is the outbreak of the Civil War. The military uprising in Gerona fails, and is followed by savage reprisals from the Anarchists and Communists, who drag their opponents from their houses under cover of darkness and shoot them without trial. Among their victims is Ignacio's younger brother, César, who is studying for the priesthood. The book ends with his death:

> A volley rang out, and César felt something gently pierce his skin.
> Moments later he heard a voice saying: "I absolve you in the name of the Father, the Son, and the Holy Ghost," ... He also heard groans. He opened his eyes for a moment. He saw a militiaman kneeling and taking tiny communion wafers from his wrist-watch and putting them into the mouths of his fallen neighbours. In the militiaman he recognized Father

Francisco. César's eyes closed. He felt a kiss on his forehead.
Then his heart stopped."

Fr. Francisco has disguised himself as a Communist militia-
man to be able to carry on his cure of souls as long as he
possibly could. Earlier on, friends have had to tie him down
to prevent him rushing out to save the sacred vessels from a
church being looted by an angry mob.

The Cypresses Believe in God is a magnificent panorama
of Spain in the thirties. The proliferation of the initials of the
various political parties—F.A.I., C.E.D.A. and so on—forces
the non-Spanish reader to keep his wits about him, but the
characters who represent these parties—El Responsable, the
Anarchist leader, Major Martínez de Soria, the leader of the
military uprising, and many others—are all unforgettable
portraits. The comparison with *War and Peace* is certainly not
far-fetched.

Other novels by Gironella are *Un hombre* ("A Man", 1946)
and *Un millón de muertes* ("A Million Deaths").

MERCEDES SALISACHS

The novels of Mercedes Salisachs provide, incidentally, a
complementary picture of Spain after the Civil War, but their
themes are universal ones. In *Una mujer llega al pueblo* ("A
Woman Arrives in the Village", 1957) (Eng. tr., *The Eyes of
the Proud*, 1960), an unmarried mother returns to her native
village on the coast of Catalonia to have her baby, but none
of the villagers except the priest and a young man once in love
with her will lift a finger to help her. The efforts of these two
are unsuccessful, and Eulalia dies. "We let her die," says Fr
Roque at Mass the next Sunday, referring to himself and his
parishioners, "and we are therefore guilty of her death. May
God have pity on us all." The unwelcome arrival of Eulalia
has shown up the villagers' religion for what it really is:
proud, loveless hypocrisy. *The Eyes of the Proud* is an
extremely skilfully organized novel; short flash-backs show us
what made these people what they are, so that the sad climax

appears as inevitable. The writing itself is distinguished: precise, economical and enlivened by a mordant humour. Eulalia is given a meal by the prudish president of the *Damas de Buena Conducta* ("Ladies of Good Conduct"), who wears plunging necklines; but she cannot keep the meal down: "Eggs ... milk. They were in her throat and her stomach heaved. In front of her all she saw was that neckline and that gap, ever whiter, ever more obsessive. It was like a basin. She opened her mouth and made use of the basin" (Trans. Delano Ames).

The Eyes of the Proud is reminiscent of some of Mauriac's attacks on false piety, but it is an earthier and more vivid book. It is also painted on a wider canvas: while Mauriac probes deeply into a small sector of society, Salisachs creates a whole community, from Communist layabout to landed proprietor, via the English tourists with their local souvenirs and stupid guffaws.

MARTÍN DESCALZO

Salisachs' picture of a Spanish village blinks no unpleasant facts, but the one painted by Martín Descalzo (b. 1930), a priest who holds the chair of literature at the seminary of Valladolid, in his novel *La frontera de Dios* (1957) (Eng. tr., *God's Frontier*, 1960), has the fierce and lurid quality of a Goya. Renato, a railway signalman who has always lived alone, re-erects a broken cross, brings a crippled child's pet canary to life and resurrects a woman. The villagers' first reaction is joy at the prospect of the profits to be made when it seems that their village is going to be a second Lourdes; but their satisfaction turns to hatred when Renato, appalled at the power given to him by God, refuses to pray for rain. He is eventually stoned to death; and the rain comes. Before his death he is confronted by the Devil, presented as an office worker with a cigarette dangling from the corner of his mouth, who says that if God were willing to do business with him he would propose a guarantee of heaven for everybody: "Then how comfortably everybody could live! Besides, it would be the way to prove to God what it is that his people want."

This penetrating study of the relationship between God and man recalls the Bernanos of *Sous le soleil de Satan* and *Monsieur Ouine*. It is the most "theological" of the Spanish novels we have discussed; Descalzo succeeds in making the spiritual and supernatural forces at work in his village as real as its sun-baked houses and fields, and Renato's death is a repetition of the crucifixion of Christ.

Other Spanish Christian novelists who have produced work of exceptional interest since the Second World War are Rafael Sánchez Mazas (*Vida nueva de Pedrito de Andía*) ("The New Life of Pedrito de Andía"), J. L. Castillo Puche (b. 1919) (*Con la muerte al hombro; Sin camino; Hicieron partes*) ("With Death as a Companion"; "Without a Path" or "Adrift"; "They Cast Lots") and Carmen Laforet (b. 1921) (*La mujer nueva*) ("The New Woman").

CHAPTER VII

PORTUGAL, SCANDINAVIA AND EASTERN EUROPE

PORTUGAL

Nuno de Montemor

Portuguese Christian writers of this century have not attracted as many translators as their Spanish colleagues, but this is the result of chance rather than of lack of merit. Fr Joaquim Augusto Álvares de Almeida (b. 1881) was a prolific writer who used the pseudonym Nuno de Montemor. His two best novels are *A Hora Vermelha* ("The Red Hour", 1932) and *Glória em Sangue* ("Glory in Blood", 1946). The former enjoyed considerable success; it is the story of a factory worker with revolutionary ideas, and could be compared with Maxence van der Meersch's novel on similar themes. Montemor's point is that his hero's complaints are largely justified and that a more sympathetic attitude on the part of employers would save a great deal of trouble. Virgilio Godinho (b. 1902), too, deals with social themes; *Calcanhar do Mundo* ("The Heel of the World") (1942) is a story of the poverty-stricken peasants of Trás-os-Montes, a backward province of northern Portugal.

Francisco Costa

In Francisco Costa's trilogy *A Garça e a Serpente* ("The Egret and the Serpent", 1943), *Revolta do Sangue* ("Revolt of the Blood", 1946) and *Cárcere Invisível* ("Invisible Prison", 1949) the focus of interest has shifted to the middle and upper classes. The hero of the trilogy, which spans nearly forty years of Portuguese life—from 1910 to the forties—eventually comes to despise the society in which he lives, breaks his ties with it and goes off to Africa as a missionary. This picture of Portuguese society has provoked comparisons with Waugh.

José Régio

The novels of the poet and critic José Régio (b. 1901) are closer to Graham Greene than to Waugh. In the trilogy *A Velha Casa*, which consists of the three novels *Uma Gota de Sangue* ("A Drop of Blood", 1945), *As Raízes do Futuro* ("The Roots of the Future", 1947) and *Os Avisos do Destino*, ("The Warning of Fate", 1953), the world is seen through the eyes of a sensitive boy called Lélito, who gradually becomes aware of the various forms that evil can assume and is enabled to come to terms with life only through religious belief. Like Graham Greene, Régio has been accused of adopting unorthodox positions.

Joaquim Paço d'Arcos

Another novelist who should be mentioned is Joaquim Paço d'Arcos (b. 1908); the heroine of *Ana Paula* (1938) is a Princesse de Clèves, a woman who refuses to desert an unworthy husband in favour of a more attractive suitor, her husband's old friend and lawyer.

José Maria Ferreira de Castro

More recently, the novelist José Maria Ferreira de Castro (b. 1898), a writer with a superb talent for accurate observation (his earlier books have been translated into most languages except English), has published an exceptionally interesting *Novelle* (or perhaps in this case we should say *Novella*) on a religious theme in *A missão* (1954) (Eng. tr., *The Mission*, 1961), which poses the whole question of the nature of religion. A community of priests in France in 1940 debates the question whether they should ensure safety from air raids for themselves—and the destruction of a factory next door—by painting "Mission" on the roof of their monastery. The twists and turns of their self-questioning are traced with a nice sensitivity.

SCANDINAVIA AND EASTERN EUROPE

Sigrid Undset

Strindberg died clutching a Bible (*Damascus* is the story of a conversion), Selma Lagerlöf often introduces Christian themes (she was a friend of Bishop Söderblom, one of the founders of the ecumenical movement) and Pär Lagerkvist has circled round Christianity (most notably in *Barabbas*), but Scandinavia's greatest Christian writer in the sense which we gave the term at the beginning of this book is unquestionably the Norwegian Sigrid Undset (1882–1949). She is one of the major figures in that twentieth-century reaction against nineteenth-century determinism which is sometimes described as a Christian renaissance.

The daughter of a well-known Norwegian archaeologist, Sigrid Undset was brought up as a Lutheran, but had drifted away from that church by the time she was due to be confirmed. One of the deciding factors, it seems, was the Lutheran church's negative attitude to chastity, which she felt should be regarded as a much more positive virtue, opening the way to spiritual development. The abandonment of Lutheranism did not lead to any particular hostility to religion, but by the time she wrote her first novel *Fru Marta Oulie* ("Mrs Marta Oulie", 1907) she was more or less an agnostic. Perhaps Marta Oulie's own words reflect the views of her creator at this time: "Seen from the inside, Christianity is consistent enough—it's like standing in a lofty cathedral with stained-glass windows. Only I know all the time that the whole real world and the daylight are outside."

This first novel of Sigrid Undset's, written at the age of twenty-five, is a novel of contemporary life. In the form of a diary, it begins with the striking words "I have been unfaithful to my husband," and is in essence an exposure of the emptiness of romantic love. Marta Oulie has lived exclusively in her love for her husband; when he ceases to interest her, her life collapses. She drifts into being unfaithful, but gains no satisfaction from it, confessing that she cared no more about her lover than she did about the mirror in her wardrobe.

Fru Marta Oulie was followed by *Den lykkelige Alder* ("The Happy Age", 1908), *Jenny* (1911; Eng. tr., *Jenny*, 1920) and *Vaaren* ("Spring", 1914), all convincing pictures of contemporary Norwegian city life (Sigrid Undset spent ten years in an office in Oslo); in so far as there is any recurrent theme or "message", it is criticism of an egotistic individualism which accepts no obligations. If the heroines of these novels fail to realize their dreams of happiness, the reason lies in themselves, not in circumstances outside them; and although *Jenny* was regarded as advanced and outspoken in its treatment of erotic experience, a great deal of emphasis is laid in these books on the sanctity of the marriage bond. *Vaaren* ends with a reconciliation between the separated Torhild and Rose. Sigrid Undset was never a feminist in the usual sense of the word; she had no time for feminine emancipation or the suffragette movement, and believed that a woman could best fulfil herself as wife and mother. "In days gone by," says Marta Oulie, "I used to get angry when I read in books that a woman was happy only when she became part of another human being. Now I say amen to this truth, just as I do to all the other outworn and shabby truths which I rejected in my youth."

There was nothing sudden about Sigrid Undset's conversion or re-conversion to Christianity, no *choc spirituel* such as Claudel experienced. She gradually came to see that Christianity embodied a number of truths which she had already experienced in her own life. Nor was it surprising that it should be Catholicism which attracted her after her youthful dissatisfaction with Lutheranism. She wrote about this time:

> The Church of Rome has at any rate form, it does not irritate the intelligence as do these diverse Protestant sects. Once poured out of the form of the Roman Church, the whole of Christianity has the effect on me of an unsuccessful, burst omelette. . . . Well, that's something else we have to thank the Germans for.

There is a vivid picture of the activities of "these diverse Protestant sects" in Selma Lagerlöf's *Jerusalem* (1901–2), in which a mystic who has returned to his native Swedish province of Dalarna from Chicago induces a whole village to sell their farms and go off to the Holy Land. Sigrid Undset had too powerful a mind to be satisfied with subjective religiosity of this sort; study and thought brought her back to Christianity, and she turned naturally to the original Church, the Church of her Norwegian forefathers. She was received into the Catholic Church on November 24th, 1924.

Sigrid Undset had always wanted to write about the Middle Ages—the very first book she wrote was a novel set in the thirteenth century, rejected by a publisher who told her to write "something modern" instead—and her growing sympathy for Catholicism gave her the point of view she needed in order to organize her material. The view generally held in Norway in the nineteenth century was that the Catholic Church had not struck deep roots in the country in the Middle Ages; it was regarded as something foreign which had merely impeded the development of the old Norse society, and the Viking Age was admired as the finest flower of the "heroic spirit of the North". In the first two decades of this century deeper study of Norwegian art and literature began to show that the old view was false; it became clear that Christianity was deeply embedded in the scaldic poetry and medieval law, and great churches like the cathedral at Trondheim were seen as solid and convincing evidence of the place occupied by Catholicism in the minds of men.

Sigrid Undset adopted the new view enthusiastically but not uncritically—the daughter of an archaeologist, she had an extremely thorough and balanced knowledge of her country's history—and gave it, as it were, artistic expression in the two great historical novels *Kristin Lavransdatter* (1920–1922; Eng. tr., *Kristin Lavransdatter*, 1930) and *Olav Audunsson* (1925–7; Eng. tr. *The Master of Hestviken*, 1928–30). Both novels are splendidly solid and vivid re-creations of medieval Norway, but they are much more than just period-pieces. The basic theme of both is that of Christianity as a whole: the idea that man is made in God's likeness and called to be God's servant and fellow-worker in the world, and that man can enjoy no happiness when his will is in conflict with that of God. In the words of St Augustine, which Eugenia Kielland used as a motto for her essays on Sigrid Undset in 1926, *Fecisti nos ad te et inquietum est cor nostrum donec requiescat in te.* The medieval period, when this conception dominated Europe, and for two or three centuries Norway formed an integral part of Europe, simply provides Sigrid Undset with the opportunity to develop her theme in its purest and fullest form. Fundamentally, both novels are books about human beings of any period; it is not fanciful to see in Kristin Lavransdatter herself a good deal of her creator.

Kristin Lavransdatter is set in the first half of the fourteenth century. In three parts, it traces the heroine's life from her childhood on her father's farm of Jorundgaard in Gudbrandsdal to her death as a nun looking after victims of the Black Death.

Kristin Lavransdatter is, as it were, the "femme moyenne sensuelle" who yet has a clear perception of the Christian ideal. When she is betrothed at the age of fifteen to Simon Darre, the son of a neighbouring farmer, she accepts the arrangement, but she is not particularly attracted by her husband-to-be and asks her father if she may spend a year in a convent at Oslo before the marriage. Lavrans, her pious and kindly father, agrees at once to this suggestion. But in Oslo Kristin meets and falls in love with the man who is to dominate her life, the charming but thoughtless Erlend Nikolausson. Kristin persuades her father to let her marry Erland instead of Simon, but by the time of the marriage she is already carrying Erlend's child and the two of them have incurred the guilt of causing the death of Erlend's mistress, Eline Ormsdatter. "Holy King Olave," Kristin prays as she kneels before the altar, "I cry to you. I pray to you for help among all the host of Heaven, for I know that above everything you loved the righteousness of God. I call on you to watch over the innocent in my womb. Turn away God's wrath from this innocent one, turn it on me, for the Lord's dear sake."

Kristin and Erlend stay together and she bears him seven sons, but she never attains again—naturally enough—the peace of mind of her childhood on her father's farm, although she rids herself of the guilt of Eline Ormsdatter's death by making a pilgrimage to St Olav's grave at Nidaros, the ancient capital of Norway, and receiving absolution for her sin from the archbishop. The description of Kristin's pilgrimage to Nidaros is one of the high-water marks of the second volume of the trilogy: "Above the green land and the magnificent city towered Christ Church, so gigantic and resplendent that everything else seemed to lie at its feet. . . . Overcome and sobbing, the young woman sank before the cross at the wayside, where thousands of pilgrims had lain and thanked God for the helping hands stretched out to mankind on the journey through this dangerous and lonely world."[1]

One of Kristin's best allies in her struggle to overcome her own temperament, and to remain true to the Christian ideal, is her husband's brother, Master Gunnulf, a man who has studied in Paris and symbolizes the links between Norway and the rest of Christendom. He becomes Kristin's close friend and exhorts her to see that her sons remain true to the covenant they made with God when they were baptized.

[1] Trans. P. G. Foote.

The three volumes of *Kristin Lavransdatter* have their *longueurs*, but all in all they form a vivid picture of the Catholic civilization of medieval Norway and, above all, a profound and balanced study of a soul's journey through life. For Sigrid Undset sees Christianity as a totality, the only intellectually satisfying and comprehensive solution to all the questions which life raises. As a wife and mother, she has a particular interest in the honourable place it accords, through Mary, to motherhood.

The themes of her second medieval novel, *Olav Audunsson*, are again those that run through all her work: love, marriage, guilt and loyalty. The tone is more sombre than that of *Kristin Lavransdatter*; the whole of Olav's life is poisoned by his secret murder of an Icelandic theological student who had seduced his wife before their marriage. He knows that only by making his peace with God can he regain his joy in life, but his pride will not let him confess his sin and make reparation for it. In other words, the book depicts the clash between the old pagan morality and the more demanding ideal of Christianity; it is a convincing picture of what must have gone on in the minds of the men of those days. Like Dostoevsky's Raskolnikov, Olav is haunted by the need for contrition, a theme which plays an important part in the work of two earlier Norwegian authors, Wergeland and Ibsen (most notably in *Peer Gynt*).

The novels of contemporary life which Sigrid Undset wrote after her conversion to Catholicism might almost be described as re-handlings of the themes of her pre-1914 novels with the Christian solution to the questions they raise firmly but not obtrusively added. In *Den trofaste husfru* (1936; Eng. tr., *The Faithful Wife*, 1937), the childless, "progressive" marriage of Nathalie and Sigurd Nordgaard breaks up because of Sigurd's affair with Adinda Gaarder. Adinda expects a child, but she is a Catholic and therefore refuses to adopt any "rational" solution to her predicament. Nathalie leaves her husband, and in turn has an affair with her old friend Sverre Reistad, whom, however, she cannot bring herself to marry. The end of the

novel is perhaps slightly too neat: Sverre Reistad dies unexpectedly, Adinda dies too, in childbirth, Sigurd brings up
her child, and he and Nathalie, who has herself adopted the
child of a dead friend, are reunited. Nathalie cannot yet bring
herself to accept the Christian faith to which Sigurd has now
returned, but the book ends with her saying, "Perhaps he
(Sigurd) is thanking the Almighty at this moment—Guardian
of all fools. . . . If he is only half as bewildered as I am,
I'm sure it must be fine to have some one to thank."

Sigrid Undset, who was awarded the Nobel prize for literature in 1928, wrote a good deal besides novels. Her political
and historical work is marked by the same honesty and vigour
as her fiction. *Et kvinnesynspunkt* ("A Woman's Point of
View", 1919), reflects her intellectual development over a
number of years; *Norske helgener* (Eng. tr., *Saga of Saints*,
1934) includes a careful and critical life of St Olav which tries
to answer the questions, "Who was St Olav?" "How did his
reputation attain such power?"; and *Etapper, ny raekke* (Eng.
tr. *Stages on the Road*, 1934) is a collection of essays, mainly
on saints, ending with a "Reply to a Parish Priest" which sums
up many of the most important aspects of its author's thought
about the significance of Christianity and its place in the
history of European civilization.

Sigrid Undset died in 1949. When it comes to the next
generation, Sweden has more to show in the way of creative
Christian writing than any of the other Scandinavian countries. The Icelander Halldor Laxness had a flirtation with
Catholicism in the twenties, but has since gone steady with
left-wing Socialism and been rewarded for his faithfulness
with the Stalin prize. The pictures of medieval churchmen in
Gerpla (1956) (Eng. tr., *The Happy Warriors*, 1958) are a
good deal more earthy than Sigrid Undset's.

Sven Stolpe

The Swede Sven Stolpe (b. 1905) started off as an exponent
of modernist literary ideas in the journal *Fronten*, but a change

of heart led him first to the Oxford Group and finally to Catholicism. The novel *Latt, enabb och öm* (Eng. tr., *Sound of a Distant Horn*, 1957) centres round a Swede called Kansdorf who is dying of cancer in Paris. A Catholic, but a lukewarm one, Kansdorf is enabled to find himself, and to die at peace with God, by two very different friends, who are themselves old acquaintances: Doctor Lebrun, a good-hearted agnostic, who is almost converted by Kansdorf's willingness to accept suffering, and Father Perezcaballero, a Dominican friar, who has had a mental breakdown. Through these three characters Stolpe looks at Christianity from three different points of view. *Sound of a Distant Horn* is not an entirely successful novel; too much of it goes on in Kansdorf's mind, which is always being invaded by romantic (and Freudian) images: "I have been hearing a remarkable thing inside me . . . a horn. And then I see a kind of Walter Scott landscape—or rather sense it, a park or something of the kind, with what looks like a woman, disappearing. An hermaphrodite, I think. I find her refreshing."[2] Lebrun's diagnosis is suppressed homosexuality; Perezcaballero's, that he must win back the love of his dead wife. We are given to understand that the second view is the correct one.

Birgitta Trotzig

In *De utsatta* ("The Exposed", 1957), Birgitta Trotzig takes us back to the seventeenth century. Isaak Graa, pastor of the village of Kirkby Tosteberga, near Christianstad in southern Sweden, is a Job-like figure who, after a lifetime of faithful service, is dispossessed of his living and all his goods on the grounds (which are quite false) that he supported the enemy when this part of Sweden was invaded by the Danes. Deserted by his son and daughter, he ends his life in the mad-house of Christianstad. The book is a powerful—not to say terrifying—evocation of the rigours of life in the seventeenth century, especially in war-time (Christianstad is twice besieged; once

[2] Trans. George Lamb.

by the Danes and once by the Swedes), but loses something through dispersal of interest. We are given, incidentally, the life-stories of the pastor's son, daughter and son-in-law; but their psychology is not credibly explained; it might have been better if the author had concentrated more continuously on the pastor himself, the Job who learns to know God through suffering, and written a *Novelle* rather than a novel. Nevertheless, the blunt, stark, biblical language of *De utsatta* and its striking imagery make it a book not quickly forgotten.

Other Swedish Novelists

Other Swedish novelists with a more or less Christian attitude are Fabian Månsson (1872–1938), whose *Rättfärdiggörelsen genom tron* ("Justification by Faith") (1916) is a half-satirical, half sympathetic commentary on the Pietism we met in Lagerlöfs *Jerusalem*; the prolific and stylish Olle Hedberg (b. 1899), who dissects the deficiencies of the middle classes and in his more recent work has shown a preoccupation with the problem of evil; and Lars Ahlin (b. 1915), an untidy but extremely fertile and creative writer in search of spiritual values. More decidedly Christian is *Klockorna i Rom* (1955; Eng. tr. *The Bells of Rome*, 1961), by Göran Stenius, a Finnish diplomat who writes in Swedish. The story of the conversion to Catholicism of a Scandinavian art historian studying in Rome, it has been described by its author (who himself became a Catholic in 1938) as "a modern legend illustrating the real presence of God in the Blessed Sacrament."

Johannes Jörgensen

The Dane Johannes Jörgensen (1866–1956), who became a Catholic in 1896, is best known for his lives of saints, especially that of St Francis of Assisi, who particularly attracted him, but he was also a lyric poet, highly regarded in Denmark, and his account of the process that led him to the Church makes a candid and moving book.

Polish authors

Apart from Wladyslaw Reymont (1867–1925), who won the Nobel prize for his four-volume novel *Chtopi* ("The Farmers", 1904–9), a Gotthelfian epic of Polish peasant life, recent Polish Catholic writers have for the most part turned to the past for their material. Antoni Golubiew (b. 1907), in *Boleslaw Chroby* (1947), another tetralogy, describes the penetration of the Slav peoples by Christianity in the eleventh century, while Jan Dobraczynski (b. 1910), who took part in the Warsaw uprising and was sent to Belsen, prefers Biblical themes. *Listy Nikodemus* (1952; Eng. tr., *The Letters of Nicodemus*, 1958) is a straightforward but moving account of the impact of Christ on Nicodemus, "a ruler of the Jews . . . (who) came to Jesus by night" (John 3, 1–2); it takes the form of letters from Nicodemus to his former tutor, Justin, which show Nicodemus torn between incredulity in this unexpected Messiah and his need to believe. Nicodemus sees the risen Christ on the road to Emmaus, and in the last letter he tells Justin that he is going off to spread Christ's message. *Swięty Miecz* (1956; Eng. tr., *The Sacred Sword*, 1959) is a novel about St Paul.

Jędrzej Giertych, who lives in exile in London, is primarily a historian, but in 1955 he published *Opowiadania Baltyckie* (Eng. tr. *Baltic Tales*, 1955), a collection of four stories about his native country which are authentic and moving pictures of Catholic Poland.

Perhaps the most original writer to emerge in Poland since the second war is Jerzy Andrzeyewski, the author of the well known *Popiol I Diament* (1957; Eng. tr., *Ashes and Diamonds*, 1962), but although two of his novels deal with religious subjects he can hardly be regarded as a Christian author. *Ciemności Kryją Ziemię* (1957; Eng. tr. *The Inquisitors*, 1957) is a potted fictional account of the Inquisition, with Torquemada undergoing a death-bed change of heart: "We must destroy what we built misguidedly at the cost of the greatest of human tragedies and sufferings . . . we must proclaim the folly of

our faith as folly and its falsehood as falsehood. It'll be necessary, my son, to learn to live without God and without Satan."[3]
The Inquisition is presented—very effectively—as a symbol
of tyranny, and although many of the leading characters in
the book besides Torquemada are priests it has little or
nothing to do with authentic Christianity. Much the same is
true of *The Gates of Paradise* (1962), a story of the Children's
Crusade written with some virtuosity (and translated into
English by James Kirkup with equal virtuosity) in only two
sentences (not counting one or two semi-colons which in effect
are full stops).

Russia

It would be surprising (*pace* Toynbee's "challenge and re-
sponse") if twentieth century Russia had much to show in
the way of Christian literature, and in fact, apart from the
philosopher Berdyaev and exiled Orthodox theologians like
Bulgakov and Florovsky, the only Christian writer of any
interest is the rather curious figure of Dimitry Merezhkovsky
(1866–1941), poet, essayist and novelist, who started off as a
protagonist of aestheticism, calling for "liberation from life
through Beauty", but soon turned to Christianity via Dostoevsky and Soloviev. His trilogy of historical novels (*Julian the
Apostate, or the Death of the Gods*, 1893; *Leonardo da Vinci,
or the Gods Resurgent*, 1896; *Peter and Alexis, or the Antichrist*, 1902), so stuffed with material from clearly recognizable
sources that Merezhkovsky was nicknamed the Napoleon of
Quotations, presents the history of Europe as a struggle between paganism and Christianity. The historical background
is painted in vivid detail, but the characters are just cardboard
figures representing ideas. Merezhkovsky's ideas tended to
remain fairly fluid. In the early years of the century he was
berating the godlessness of Russian intellectuals and defend-
ing the Orthodox Church; after the revolution of 1905 he was
calling it a "stronghold of reaction". His mystical leanings led

[3] Trans. Konrad Syrop.

him to propound some very curious ideas, among them the Platonic notion that the answer to mankind's imperfections and limitations was the hermaphrodite. He left Russia after the October revolution and went to live in Paris. He called the Communists the servants of Antichrist, wrote a defence of Mussolini and welcomed Hitler's invasion of Russia as a "crusade against the enemies of mankind". During his exile he produced a spate of books; most of them are rhetorical and verbose, and none of them equals in interest or vigour the "Christ and Antichrist" trilogy.

EPILOGUE

Large though the number of writers mentioned in this little book has been, there would have been plausible grounds for including even more. For instance, if the Greek Nikos Kazantzakis (1882–1957) was clearly not a Christian, he was equally certainly concerned with questions that can fairly be described as religious, and his novel *Christ Recrucified* (Eng. tr., 1954) is a skilful and moving transposition of the story of Christ into a modern Anatolian setting. Another novel which it would have been interesting to analyse is the American William Gaddis's lengthy *The Recognitions* (1952). But the line had to be drawn somewhere and, even as it is, the extent of the ground I have tried to cover has prevented anything but a swift and superficial treatment of most of the writers discussed.

There are just two further points which I should like to make. I argued in the introduction that there is indeed such a thing as Christian literature, and I hope that the book as a whole has lent some colour to the assertion, but those who would deny it can certainly quote in their support no less eminent a Christian and scholar than Cardinal Newman, who said in *Duties of the Church Towards Philosophy*[1]: "... if Literature is to be made a study of human nature, you cannot have a Christian Literature. It is a contradiction in terms to attempt a sinless Literature of sinful man. You may gather together something very great and high, something higher than any literature ever was; and when you have done so, you will find that it is not Literature at all." The answer to

[1] The tenth of his *Discourses on the Scope and Nature of University Education* (1852).

this is twofold. First, in this context (he was arguing in favour of the inclusion of literature as a whole in the curriculum of Christians being prepared to face the world), Newman had in mind something different from the kind of literature discussed in this book. For Newman, "Christian literature" conjured up a picture of bowdlerized, "sinless" productions deliberately intended to edify: here, the term has been used simply to describe literature written from a Christian standpoint. Second, peculiarly interesting though this kind of literature must be to Christians, I have not suggested that they should neglect other kinds. Literature, like truth, is indivisible, and Christians, being men, cannot arbitrarily neglect any part of it. Their only duty is not to forget, in their reading, that they are Christians. As Newman put it further on in the same discourse, "(The Church's) principle is one and the same throughout: not to prohibit truth of any kind, but to see that no doctrines pass under the name of Truth but those which claim it rightfully".

SELECT BIBLIOGRAPHY

General

GLASER, Hermann: *Kleine Geschichte der modernen Weltliteratur. Dargestellt in Problemkreisen*, Frankfurt/M., Ullstein Taschenbücher Verlag, 3rd enlarged ed., 1960.

KERMODE, Frank: *Puzzles and Epiphanies; Essays and Reviews, 1958–1961*, London, Routledge and Kegan Paul, and New York, Chilmark Press, 1962. (Contains essays on Allen Tate, Graham Greene, Evelyn Waugh and William Golding.)

KRANZ, Gisbert: *Europas Christliche Literatur, 1500–1960*, Aschaffenburg, Paul Pattloch Verlag, 1961. (The only complete survey of the subject; comprehensive, but at times necessarily cursory.)

O'DONNELL, Donat (Pseudonym of Conor Cruise O'Brien): *Maria Cross: Imaginative Patterns in a Group of Catholic Writers*, London and New York, Oxford Univ. Press, 1953; new edition, with fresh introduction and appendices, London, Burns and Oates, 1963. (The writers discussed include Bernanos, Claudel, Mauriac, Waugh and Greene.)

TURNELL, Martin: *Modern Literature and Christian Faith*, London, Darton, Longman and Todd, and Westminster, Md, Newman Press, 1961.

England

In the series of booklets entitled *Writers and Their Work*, published by Longmans, London, New York and Toronto, for the British Council and the National Book League, there are essays on Hilaire Belloc (by Renée Haynes), G. K. Chesterton (by Christopher Hollis), Ford Madox Ford (by Kenneth Young), T. S. Eliot (by M. C. Bradbrook), Graham Greene (by Francis Wyndham), Evelyn Waugh (by Christopher Hollis) and Charles Williams (by J. Heath Stubbs). Each booklet contains a fairly complete bibliography and a short list of critical studies.

DAICHES, David: *The Present Age: After 1920* (Introductions to English Literature, Vol. V), London, Cresset Press, and Bloomington, Indiana, Indiana Univ. Press, 1958.

FORD, Boris (editor): *The Pelican Guide to English Literature*, Vol. 7, *The Modern Age*, Harmondsworth and Baltimore, Penguin Books, 1961.

SPEAIGHT, Robert: *The Life of Hilaire Belloc*, London, Hollis and Carter, and New York, Farrar, Straus and Cudahy, 1957.

BELLOC, Hilaire: *The Place of Chesterton in English Letters*, London, Sheed and Ward, 1940, and New York, Sheed and Ward, 1941.

O'CONNOR, Monsignor J.: *Father Brown on Chesterton*, London, Burns and Oates, and Toronto, S. J. R. Saunders, 1937.

WARD, Maisie: *Gilbert Keith Chesterton*, New York, Sheed and Ward, 1943, and London, Sheed and Ward, 1944.

LOVAT, Laura: *Maurice Baring: A Postscript with Some Letters and Verse*, London, Hollis and Carter, 1947, and New York, Sheed and Ward, 1948.

WAUGH, Evelyn: *The Life of Ronald Knox*, London, Chapman and Hall, 1959; Collins, Fontana Books, 1962.

GARDNER, Helen: *The Art of T. S. Eliot*, London, Cresset Press, and New York, Dutton, 1950.

MATTHIESEN, F. O.: *The Achievement of T. S. Eliot*, 3rd edn, with a chapter on Eliot's later work by C. L. Barber, London and New York, Oxford University Press, 1958.

ELIOT, T. S.: "The Significance of Charles Williams," in *The Listener*, 19 December, 1946.

RIDLER, Anne (editor): *Charles Williams: The Image of the City and Other Essays*, London and New York, Oxford Univ. Press, 1958. (A selection of essays prefaced by a critical introduction.)

WINTHROP, G. P., Jr.: "This Rough Magic," in *The Yale Review*, Cambridge, Mass., Winter 1950. (Deals with Williams's novels.)

DE VITIS, A. A.: *Roman Holiday: The Catholic Novels of Evelyn Waugh*, New York, Bookman Associates, 1956.

STOPP, F. J.: *Evelyn Waugh: Portrait of an Artist*, London, Chapman and Hall, and Boston, Little, Brown, 1958.

WILSON, Edmund: "Never Apologize, Never Explain," in the *New Yorker*, 4 March, 1944; reprinted in *Classics and Commercials*, New York, Farrar, Straus and Cudahy, 1950, and London, W. H. Allen, 1951, pp. 140–6.

ALLOTT, K., and FARRIS, M.: *The Art of Graham Greene*, London, Hamish Hamilton, and Toronto, British Book Service, 1951.

MESNET, M-B.: *Graham Greene and the Heart of the Matter*, London, Cresset Press, 1954 (Deals mainly with *Brighton Rock*, *The Power and the Glory* and *The Heart of the Matter*).

America

CUNLIFFE, Marcus: *The Literature of the United States*, Harmondsworth and Baltimore, Penguin Books, 1954.

GARDINER, Harold C., S. J. (editor): *Fifty Years of the American Novel: a Christian Appraisal*, London and New York, Scribner's, 1951. (A collection of essays by Catholic critics on a number of modern American novelists, from Edith Wharton to Norman Mailer. Francis Connolly, writing on Willa Cather, takes the curious but interesting view that she "(may never have) properly understood the Christian spirituality which is the informing principle of *Death Comes for the Archbishop* and *Shadows on the Rock*".)

GEISMAR, Maxwell: *The Last of the Provincials: The American Novel,
1915–1925*, London, Secker and Warburg, and Boston, Houghton,
Mifflin, 1947. (Includes chapters on Willa Cather and Scott Fitzgerald.)

GEISMAR, Maxwell: *American Moderns*, London, W. H. Allen, and
New York, Hill and Wang, 1958 (has a chapter on John Howard
Griffin).

GORDON, Caroline, and TATE, Allen (editors): *The House of Fiction:
an Anthology of the Short Story*, New York, Scribner's, 2nd edn,
1960. (An anthology of short stories with a commentary on each.
The stories include Faulkner's *Spotted Horses*, Powers's *Lions,
Harts, Leaping Does* and Flannery O'Connor's *A Good Man is
Hard to Find*. The commentary on *Spotted Horses* suggests that
Flem Snopes may be regarded as the Devil. This would seem to
be reading into the text rather more than is actually there.)

HERZBERG, Max (editor): *The Reader's Encyclopedia of American
Literature*, New York, Thomas Y. Crowell, and London,
Methuen, 1963. (Covers Canadian as well as American literature.)

HOFFMAN, Frederick C.: *The Modern Novel in America. 1900–1950*;
Chicago, Regnery, 1951.

MAXWELL, D. E. S.: *American Fiction. The Intellectual Background*,
London, Routledge and Kegan Paul and New York, Columbia
University Press, 1963.

BENNETT, Mildred R.: *The World of Willa Cather*, New York, Dodd
Mead, 1951.

BLOOM, Edward A. and Lillian D.: *Willa Cather's Gift of Sympathy*,
Carbondale, Southern Illinois University Press, 1962. (Very good
on the genesis and composition of the novels.)

BROWN, E. K., completed by Edel, Leon: *Willa Cather: A Critical
Biography*, New York, Knopf, 1953.

DAICHES, David: *Willa Cather: A Critical Introduction*, Ithaca, Cornell
University Press, 1951.

TATE, Allen (editor): *A Southern Vanguard*, New York, Prentice-Hall,
1947. (Includes an interesting essay on Faulkner by Malcolm
Cowley.)

France

BRÉE, Germaine, and GUITON, Margaret: *An Age of Fiction. The
French Novel from Gide to Camus*, London, Chatto and Windus,
1958, and New Brunswick (N.J.), Rutgers University, 1957.

BRÉE, Germaine and others: *What's Novel in the Novel*, Yale French
Studies Number Eight, New Haven, Conn., Yale University Press,
1952. (Includes essays on Bernanos and Cayrol.)

BROMBERT, Victor: *The Intellectual Hero. Studies in the French Novel,
1880–1955*, London, Faber and Faber, 1962. (Includes discussions
of Bourget and Malègue.)

CRUICKSHANK, John (editor): *The Novelist as Philosopher. Studies in French Fiction, 1935–1960*, London and New York, Oxford University Press, 1962. (Includes a chapter on Bernanos by E. Beaumont and one on Cayrol by Carlos Lynes.)

FOWLIE, WALLACE: *Guide to Contemporary French Literature, from Valéry to Sartre*, New York, Meridian Books, 1957.

HEPPENSTALL, Rayner: *The Fourfold Tradition. Notes on the French and English Literatures, with Some Ethnological and Historical Asides*, London, Barrie and Rockliff, 1961. (Discusses Bernanos and Mauriac.)

MAUGENDRE, L.-A.: *La Renaissance catholique au début du XXe siècle*, Paris, Beauchesne, 1963.

PEYRE, Henri: *The Contemporary French Novel*, New York, Oxford Univ. Press, 1955.

SIMON, Pierre-Henri: *Histoire de la littérature française au XXe siècle, 1900–1950*, Paris, Armand Colin, 1956.

TURNELL, Martin: *The Art of French Fiction*, London, Hamish Hamilton, 1959. (Includes a section on Mauriac.)

FOWLIE, Wallace: *Claudel (Studies in Modern European Literature and Thought)*, Cambridge, Bowes and Bowes, and New York, Hillary House, 1958.

FOWLIE, Wallace: *Clowns and Angels*, London and New York, Sheed and Ward, 1943.

CHAIGNE, Louis: *Georges Bernanos*, Paris, Éditions Universitaires, 3rd edn, 1960.

JARRETT-KERR, M. (C. R.): *François Mauriac (Studies in Modern European Literature and Thought)* Cambridge, Bowes and Bowes, and New Haven, Conn., Yale Univ. Press, 1954.

ROBICHON, J.: *François Mauriac*, Paris, Éditions Universitaires, 1953.

SIMON, Pierre-Henri: *Mauriac par lui-même*, Paris, Éditions du Seuil, 1953.

BRODIN, Pierre: *Julien Green*, Paris, Éditions Universitaires, 1957.

CAIN, Seymour: *Gabriel Marcel (Studies in Modern European Literature and Thought)*, Cambridge, Bowes and Bowes, and New York, Hillary House, 1963.

Germany

BITHELL, Jethro: *Modern German Literature, 1880–1950*, 3rd revised edn, London, Methuen, 1959.

FRIEDMANN, Hermann, and MANN, Otto (editors): *Christliche Dichter der Gegenwart*, Heidelberg, 1955.

GLASER, Hermann, LEHMANN, Jakob, and LUBOS, Arno: *Wege der deutschen Literatur. Eine geschichtliche Darstellung*, Frankfurt/M. and Berlin, Verlag Ullstein, 1961.

LANGE, Victor: *Modern German Literature 1870–1940*, Ithaca, New York, 1945.

WAIDSON, H. M.: *The Modern German Novel. A Mid-Twentieth Century Survey*, London and New York, Oxford Univ. Press for the University of Hull, 1959.

JAPPE, Hajo: *Gertrud von le Fort. Das erzählende Werk*, Meran, Verlag Hermann Unterberger, no date.

HILTON, I.: "Gertrud von le Fort—A Christian Writer", in *German Life and Letters*, Vol. XV, no. 4, July 1962.

Italy

WHITFIELD, J. H.: *A Short History of Italian Literature*, Harmondsworth and Baltimore, Penguin Books, 1960.

WILKINS, Ernest Hatch: *A History of Italian Literature*, London and New York, Oxford Univ. Press, 1954.

NARDI, P.: *Antonio Fogazzaro*, Milan, 1938.

Spain

BALLESTER, Gonzalo T.: *Panorama de la Literatura Española Contemporánea*, Madrid, Ediciones Guadarrama, 1956.

EOFF, Sherman H.: *The Modern Spanish Novel*, London, Peter Owen, 1962, and New York, New York University Press, 1961.

BAREA, Arturo (trans. by Ilsa Barea): *Unamuno* (*Studies in Modern European Literature and Thought*), Cambridge, Bowes and Bowes, and New Haven, Connecticut, Yale University Press, 1952.

Portugal

AMEAL, J.: *Panorama de la littérature portugaise contemporaine*, 1948.

LE GENTIL, G.: *La Littérature portugaise*, 2 Vol., 1951.

Scandinavia and Eastern Europe

BEYER, Harald: *A History of Norwegian Literature*, New York, New York University Press, 1956.

DYBOSKI, Roman: *Modern Polish Literature*, London and New York, Oxford Univ. Press. 1924.

GUSTAFSON, Alrik: *A History of Swedish Literature*, Minneapolis, University of Minnesota Press, 1961.

MIRSKY, D. S.: *A History of Russian Literature*, ed. and abridged by F. J. Whitfield, London, Routledge and Kegan Paul, and New York, Alfred A. Knopf, 1949.

MITCHELL, P. M.: *A History of Danish Literature*, Copenhagen, Gyldendal, in conjunction with the American-Scandinavian Foundation, 1957.

PIETRKIEWICZ, Jerzy: *Polish Prose and Verse. A Selection with an Introductory Essay*, London, University of London, Athlone Press, 1956.

WINSNES, A. H.: *Sigrid Undset: A Study in Christian Realism*, trans. by P. G. Foote, London and New York, Sheed and Ward, 1953.

Credo, a quarterly review published by the Jesuits at Uppsala, reviews most of the books written by modern Catholic Scandinavian authors.